Let Your Angels Lead

Connecting with your angels for freedom from fear and stress

Ivory LaNoue

SEDONA VIBRATIONS PUBLISHING

Copyright © 2021 by Ivory LaNoue

First Edition published November 2021

Second Edition published August 2023

Sedona Vibrations Publishing

Contact: SedonaVibrationsPublishing@outlook.com

ISBN: 9798487161406

All rights reserved.

No portion of this book may be reproduced in any form without written permission from the publisher or author, except as permitted by U.S. copyright law.

Dedication

This book is dedicated to my angels for their unwavering guidance, love and for pushing me to write this book. Particular thanks to my Master Guide, Marius, as he would not stop bringing my attention back to this project, no matter what was going on in my life. Thank you to my daughter Michelle, my soul sisters Rozlyn and Terri-Ann, my brother Allen, parents Henry and Wilda, and Spence. All of you encouraged me and kept me motivated through the writing process. My sincere gratitude to my mediumship mentor, Susanne Wilson, who took me on as her student at a very low point in my life and injected light back into my world.

Foreword

Now, perhaps more than ever, there is a deep thirst for a better connection with intuitive intelligence and infinite love. In Let Your Angels Lead, Ivory LaNoue has gifted us with the keys to accessing our angels every day, and, bet of all, anyone can do it!

Having previously mentored Ivory in mediumship studies, I knew for a face that she was an excellent medium, one of the best I had seen. However, the fun part is that I am also highly clairvoyant. This means that I can see subtle energies. Wow! I have never seen Ivory without her ever-present group of beautiful angels surrounding her. Naturally, when I heard that she was writing a book, I had hoped to be asked to write the foreword. I am confident that Let Your Angels Lead will be a life-changing book for anyone fortunate enough to read it.

I have also been aware of how successfully Ivory's students have utilized her methods for angel communication. This comes as no surprise. I know of nobody more experienced and passionate about teaching angel communication in a way that anyone can learn and put into practice.

Do you have any personal experiences with angels? Were there "imaginary friends" around you during childhood? Listen, early childhood experiences are not a prerequisite for you to be successful in communicating with angels. However, it is remarkable that Ivory has been in touch with angels since she was a toddler and vividly remembers these early events. In fact, I thoroughly enjoyed her true-life accounts of angels interspersed through the book. The personal stories practically leap from the pages to touch your heart. Ivory's literary voice is compelling and engaging; do not start this book late at night, or you will be aware past the darn.

If you have ever experienced an extremely low point such as major depression, this book may help you avoid going down the wrong path again. It may also prevent you from suffering more than is truly necessary. I say this because suffering does seem to be part of the experience of being human. However, as Ivory has said, no one should ever get stuck within a "dark night of the soul." She is not wrong about that! When you realize how angels communicate, you can call upon them at any time for comfort and guidance. You will learn to receive their messages during your sorrows as well as your celebrations. The angels are but a heartbeat away. You simply need to know how they work.

In sum, Let Your Angels Lead is my number one recommendation. It is easy to use, and it is fun to read. All the work has already been done for you! You can receive clear guidance, comfort, and validations of your inner wisdom with this book. If not now, when?

Susanne J. Wilson, MPA, and the Carefree Medium; intuition educator and author of Soul Smart: What the Dead Teach Us About Spirit Communication

carefreemedium.com

Introduction

We were one month into awareness of COVID-19 in the United States. On an April night in 2020, I began my daily intentions and spiritual protection when I felt something hit me in the upper stomach. It took me to my knees on the floor, where I stayed for a few minutes, trying to breathe and waiting for the pain to subside. I remember shaking and being frightened because I had no idea what was happening.

The next day I was exhausted and found it challenging to think clearly. It was so bad, I rescheduled my clients as I couldn't do my work within a clear hear. I spent the day resting, drinking a lot of water, and wondering if I was getting sick.

I could not imagine what this was, but then my clients, who are empaths, began reaching out to me for help. They were being hit by similar waves, feeling depleted of energy and a sense of being numb. That was when I realized that the level of negative energy around the planet, caused by fear, anger, and stress was even more damaging than I had thought.

Empaths are people who pick up on other people's feelings, including the emotions of the planet when a strong emotion overrides that of others. The Solar Plexus chakra, the upper stomach, is the most prominent receptor in the human body of energy and emotions. Though I do daily protection to keep myself from feeling other's emotions outside of sessions, this tsunami of fear had hit me hard.

I experienced that overwhelming wave of feelings two more times before my angels came in to talk with me about the situation. They verified that it was entirely due to the negative energy permeating our planet. My angels told me that I would require extra protection during this time to avoid being completely overpowered by this destructive energy.

So, I tripled my daily protection, reduced my time around people I found difficult as I knew they would add to the negative effect, and isolated myself at home to manage my energetic environment. At first, I found this to be very difficult. I was lonely, feeling disconnected from my family, workmates, and friends. However, this plan proved successful within a few weeks. I felt well enough to instruct my clients and students on what they could do to stop feeling that massive wave of fear.

These moments of being brought down by the negative feelings around the world were a big wake-up call for me. I knew that I had a choice of sinking into the abyss of fear and stress or doing what it took to rise above it. I chose to rise. Accomplishing this would not have been possible without the loving assistance from my angels.

When a significant event impacts a family, it is stressful. When it affects the whole world, the stress and fear turn into a dense layer of energy that is difficult to rise above. Right now, between COVID-19, the collapse of economies, and general unrest, we have a lot of negative energy to push through.

Add to that all the stressors each person is experiencing on a day-to-day basis, outside of world chaos. All of this has created fear. At its core, stress is about fear. Because when you are stressed, you are afraid of what has happened or what might happen.

When a person is in a situation like this, they are not thinking straight. It is hard to make decisions, use intuition or discernment, or even know what is true. Recognizing that one of your angels is speaking to you or surrounding you in their beautiful angelic energy is incredibly comforting and calming.

Most people slog through their days as best as possible, doing what they did before. But there is an entire realm of assistance available to you that can lift your frequency, leading you to feel a lot better and rise above the stress and fear.

The problem is that most people don't know how to connect to that help. I have created a program of tapping into that support, so you don't have to try to find your way through these crazy times by yourself.

You already know that angels exist, and you feel a connection to them. Or you are curious and open to learning more about them. I understand that. Life can be scary sometimes but know that you don't have to go through your challenges alone.

Before they gained a firm grasp on the level of love, protection, and guidance available to them from their angels, my clients were afraid, worrying a lot, feeling lost and isolated. However, through connecting with their angels with my help, they now face uncertainty with calm, frightening circumstances with trust and rarely feel worried.

You will learn that there are two ways of communicating with your angels. One is through daily communications and requests. The other is for times when you are in crisis, terrified, quite frozen in indecision. You will learn more about that later in this book.

The angels say that our world is at a significant pivotal point right now. We can propel ourselves forward into enlightenment, peace, abundance, and love. But if enough people do not reduce their fear, we could move away from the light and into further darkness. So, we have a choice and the ability to turn things around and help ourselves. This, in turn, helps the world.

The purpose of this book is to guide you through connecting with your angels on a deep level, resulting in you having a real relationship with them. Reading this book will help you get to that place as quickly as possible. Being aware of the presence of your angels allows you to trust that you have protection and guidance. With this knowledge, you can overcome anxiety and fear. This will help you feel more calm, clear-headed, and positive.

You will learn why your angels feel it is critical you have a close bond with them at this time. In Chapter 3, my angels will explain that in their own words. They let you know about the beautiful worldwide changes to expect as more people come to trust that angels exist and they get to know their angels. You and many others will overcome the lower frequencies of fear and stress, creating a more light and joyful world.

Just as important, you can expect concrete methods of feeling, seeing, and hearing your angels. I will guide you through exercises that help you achieve all forms of angelic connection, no matter what your skill level is currently.

Indeed, some will more easily feel angels or see them. Others will struggle with that. Most people have internal barriers which prevent them from experiencing angelic contact. It's not usually a conscious decision to put those barriers up, and there is no set time for how long it will take for them to come down. But, if you keep up with the exercises in this book, you will succeed. I have included a Troubleshooting chapter to help you push past those barriers if you have difficulty.

Please do not compare yourself to anyone else. Everyone is unique in how they progress. I'm a firm believer that persistence is a crucial element to success in any endeavor, including angelic communication.

I have explained how to interpret these methods of communication so you can make use of them. Otherwise, it would be much like reading a French book without knowing the language.

Knowing this information increases your awareness of the possibilities. It will be a lot less likely that you would miss a message, sign, or symbol.

Included is information about why it's so important to follow the guidance of your angels. You will read some examples of what happened to me and others when we preferred our chosen path over the one our angels guided us to take.

I hope to prevent you from making similar mistakes. By taking that chapter to heart, you can avoid unnecessary trauma and chaos, both literally and emotionally, throughout the rest of your life.

You will learn how to keep a journal on your deepening relationship with your angels. This book will teach you how to do this in a way that helps you remember messages, guidance, and what you have seen. You will know how to keep track of your practice sessions, and see the progress you have made.

Reading this book will teach you how to receive specific, powerful intervention from your angels when you are worried, frightened, or in need.

Knowing how to call on this urgent angelic aid can prevent you from going into a prolonged dark period of life or begin the process of pulling out of one. If you have gone through a Dark Night of the Soul, you know how difficult it is to climb out of an emotional pit. However, these huge setbacks can be avoided or shortened.

You will learn details about how angels appear when they are actively protecting you. This information will give you tremendous peace, knowing that one of the most potent forces for good and light is on the job, keeping you safe.

Soon, you will realize that you are never alone, nor are you dealing with life's difficulties by yourself. You will come to understand that you have a genuine connection to angels and that is life changing.

You may be wondering, "Why should I listen to this lady?" or "Who is this Ivory person?" I was born with a strong connection to angels. I saw, felt and heard them on a regular basis. It was a long journey to pursue this work full-time, but I got here. First, I had a career in radio, where the public service promotions I created earned a Crystal Award for the radio station. This is one of the top awards given in radio. It is for excellence in year-round community service. Then my angels guided me to shift into working in the field of mental health for low-income and homeless persons. I did that for a long time, ending my career as Program Coordinator for the mental health program for a county in central Arizona.

I have taught this angelic communication program to thousands of people from all over the world. Most of my business is word-of-mouth and referral. I stay busy, and am passionate about my work, which is my life's purpose.

My clients often contact me to share their personal stories of angel contact, awareness, and messages. I did not create this program; my angels did. All credit goes to them for urging me to share this information with my clients and in this book.

I want you to feel comfortable with me. So, if you wish to know more about me, visit my website and read my reviews on sites like Yelp, Trip Advisor and Google. My website is listed on the About the Author page.

Let me dispel any illusions that I am an angel or a perfect person. Not at all. I have faults and make mistakes. I'm a mother and a grandmother. I pay bills, visit family, do laundry, socialize with friends, and do grocery shopping like everyone else. I'm just an average person who happens to have a strong connection with angels.

In the chapters of this book, I'm going to teach you about:

- The different ways angels appear
- The value of keeping an angel journal
- How to feel, see and hear your angels
- Overcoming barriers that are keeping you from achieving angelic communication skills
- Developing a close relationship with your angels
- Recognizing angelic guidance and how it appears
- What Angel People are
- How going rogue is a bad idea
- Recovering from a Dark Night of the Soul
- Receiving extra angelic assistance when in crisis
- Releasing fear and stress
- Knowing what angelic protection looks like

There are some other benefits you are likely to gain simply by interacting with your angels. Their incredibly high frequency lifts yours and changes you in beautiful ways.

Angels are wondrous beings of light, wisdom, peace, and love. They are God's messengers. When one of your angels is aware of you feeling a negative emotion such as sadness, grief, fear, loneliness, being unloved, or depression, they wish to help you move out of that emotion.

Having your angels focused on you and your feelings evokes a profound sense of being loved, feeling peace, emotional tranquility, and harmony within. This change will come upon you suddenly, and you may wonder why you feel so much better.

Accept it as a sign of the deep love and caring your angels have you for always. They hurt when they see you are suffering.

Having this incredible angelic energy surrounding you can leave you feeling loved unconditionally. Maybe for the first time in your life. You may feel highly comforted, at ease, as if all is well in your life. Nothing has changed in your life or around you. These changes are all within, and they can be lasting.

You may find that you look at the world differently. You begin seeing the good in people, the beautiful in nature, and feeling love for all humanity. Your ability for love and compassion is expanded dramatically. Quite simply, you are not who you were before this sign occurred.

It is unlikely that you will feel anything but relief and joy about these changes when you experience them.

I want to help you start your journey of getting to know your angels in a way that gives you the best chance of succeeding.

Getting Started

Do a short meditation, say a prayer, or do some chanting before reading further in this book. I suggest you read one chapter and then give yourself three to seven days to absorb the information and practice the exercises. Then continue to the next chapter.

If you get stuck on feeling, seeing, or hearing your angels, refer to the Troubleshooting section to work on breaking through any barriers.

Let me introduce you to my world. A life where I feel, hear and see my angels often. Guidance is there for those seeking it. I know I am never alone and soon, you will have that same knowing.

Table of Contents

1. My Glowing Friends — 1
   Don't Drink the Smoothies
   Inspiration
   Birth of a Book
   Such a Vivid Imagination
   Angel Experiences
   I See Angels

2. I'm a Medium! — 9
   Moment of Revelation
   It Took So Long
   Signs
   Honing Gifts
   Use it For Yourself

3. From My Angels to You — 17
   Connect With Your Angels
   My Angels Speak

4. Keeping an Angel Journal — 21
   Send me the Right People
   Why it's Helpful
   So Many Choices
   Info to Include
   Format
   Getting Started

      Improving Spiritual Gifts
      Get Out of Your Own Way

5. Feeling Your Angels   31
      I Just Killed Them All
      Surprising Sensation
      Use Your Senses
      Let's Get Ready
      Feeling Your Master Guide
      Feeling an Archangel
      Feeling Other Angels on Your Team
      Emotions Rule

6. Seeing Your Angels   43
      What's Up With the Lights?
      What Angels Look Like
      How to See Your Angels
      Seeing Your Master Guide
      Seeing Your Guardian Angel
      Seeing Other Angels on Your Team
      The Big Dream
      Take Your Time

7. Hearing Your Angels   53
      Plenty of Toilet Paper
      Where Did That Come From?
      So Annoying!
      Qualities to Expect
      Ringing Ears
      Music
      Behind the Scenes
      Developing Trust
      Exercises

8. Scent of Angels   65

Clairalience
When it Happens
Stop and Smell the Roses
Difficult to Describe
Angelic Scents
Associated Feelings
Using Scent to Communicate With Angels
Exercises

9. Troubleshooting   73
You Can't Force This
Breaking Barriers
Lift Your Spirits
Clearing with Essential Oils
Open Those Chakras
Exercises
Meditation
Raise Your Frequency
It's Working
Affirmations

10. Angels in Your Heart   87
Stepping Out of Fear
Angel Shapes
Angels Have Longings
Great Expectations
Bonding Time
Free Will
Asking for Intervention
Greeting Them
Exercises
Angelic Personalities
Creating Angelic Space

11. Guidance From Your Angels — 99
    Warning!
    Easily Overlooked
    Angelic Communications
    Spoken Word
    Not Always Welcome
    Transformation Time
    Signs

12. Angel People — 123
    Divine Realm Connection
    Humans, Not Angels
    Recognizing This Gift
    Use it for Yourself

13. Going Rogue — 129
    His Mother Warned Me
    Going What?
    A Really Bad Idea
    Dark Night of the Soul
    Signs You Are in One
    Out of the Pit
    Find a Spiritual Circle.
    Exercises

14. Parade of Angels — 147
    Spectacular Protection
    Crisis Assistance
    Requesting Help
    Seeing Angelic Protection
    Exercises
    Fountain of Joy

Dear Reader — 155

Celestial Connections	157
Contact Ivory LaNoue	159
About the Author	161

CHAPTER ONE
My Glowing Friends

Don't Drink the Smoothies

I had entered a relationship with a man we'll call "John", who had presented himself as a spiritual person. He said the right things, but occasionally it was like a mask slipped, and I glimpsed an aspect of him I did not like. Yet, being a Lightworker, I saw his positive qualities. I wanted to believe his tales of being used and emotionally abused in past relationships. "John" had such potential as a person, and I believe he could reach it.

I had left behind a long-term career, the Celtic band I sang with, an active social life, and my hometown to move to the Phoenix area with John. All of this added to my determination to make the relationship work. But, over time, "John's" mask slips increased, and my sense of unease that I may have made the worst mistake of my life grew. Regularly I was receiving messages from my angels. They told me, "He is not in your best and highest good," telling me to look in a specific place for evidence of his behavior and letting me know that "everything will be alright."

Yet, I stayed in the hopes of helping "John" leave his dark past and addictive behaviors behind. I knew this was not the right decision for me. Eventually, the long-term stress took its toll, and my health went downhill. For 111 days I experienced unexplained bleeding. My GYN could find no reason for this. Finally, another doctor did lab work and found that my liver and kidneys were losing function. I felt my life source fading. Not only was my spirit suffering, but my physical health was as well.

My angels warned me not to drink the smoothies my boyfriend was bringing home to me. I thought I was being paranoid. After all, this was a man who said he loved me. "John" knew I enjoyed those smoothies, and I thought it was sweet that he was getting them for me. My thinking was, "Surely he would never do anything to hurt me." So, I drank a few more of them. Unfortunately, my health went further downhill. Eventually, the bleeding stopped.

A few months went by, and the bleeding started again. This time it continued for 91 days. Though I had asked "John" not to bring me smoothies, he did most of the cooking for us. That left me continuing to be vulnerable.

I had exploratory surgery, and my surgeon found nothing to explain the bleeding. My angels told me there had been something in the smoothies "John" brought me that made me sick. I distinctly heard, "Don't drink the smoothies." The part of me that believed I could help "John" had take precedent over self-preservation. I asked my angels to give me an unmistakable sign telling me what to do.

This book will tell you about the powerful dream I had were all my angels were surrounding me. After that dream, I knew what I had to do to save myself and shift my life forward in a positive direction. When the relationship with "John" ended, I was able to heal on every level.

My organs went back to a healthy function within four months. I could see the situation clearly and get help for the mental and emotional abuse I had suffered. My circle of support was astounded by how fast I healed.

It's fantastic what angels can help you accomplish.

Inspiration

A year later, my angels came to tell me I needed to create a *Meet Your Angelic Guides* session. They told me this session was meant to connect people with their angels and guides. It needed to include the names and appearances of the angels and guides and personal messages from them for my clients. I could feel a sense of urgency from them about this new session.

I asked why this session was necessary. My angels were silent. But I had long ago learned that I needed to follow their guidance right away. So, over a few days, I put the session together and added it to my website. Immediately I began getting a lot of bookings for this session. People wrote to tell me that following their session with me, they felt the presence of their angels. They were seeing them, or hearing them, and gaining from the connection they were creating. I had my answer.

Birth of a Book

Seven years ago, my angels were urging me to write a book. At the time, they did not specify what the purpose of this would be. My angels may have been giving me other messages which I missed because my dear friend, Tony, had died suddenly, my lengthy toxic relationship with John was grinding to a painful end, and my health was poor. I told my angels that I was in no positive to write a book at that time.

As the years passed, my angels began talking to me more urgently about this book. When the pandemic hit, they said, "This book needs to be available now." I tried explaining that it would take time to write it, but they continued pushing me to hurry and get it out. That is the reason I decided to self-publish. My angels and I are focused on giving people access to this information as quickly as possible.

My angels guided me through the entire process of writing this book. Before each writing session, I would ask my angels to give me the words they wanted to share. They helped me know what to write to open hearts and minds, and encourage people to begin building a close relationship with their angels. All credit for my session and this book goes to my beautiful angelic team.

Such a Vivid Imagination

When I was two years old, my family lived in the countryside town of Urbana, Maryland. My father had remodeled an old one-room schoolhouse for our home. It still had the school bell in a tower on the roof.

I could play outside most of the day, and my mother was close at hand hanging laundry or watching over my younger sister and I. At this time, my sister, Dee was a little over a year old, so our mother had her hands full. However, I was inquisitive even then and wandered off the property and down a dirt road.

It was in the afternoon. It felt like I walked for a long time, but I am sure it was not, or my mom would have been frantically searching the neighborhood. I did not know where I was and was standing in the middle of the dirt road, feeling frightened.

I heard a woman's soft voice speak to me. I turned around. At the top of a hill, I saw a beautiful, glowing lady with long light red hair, pale skin, a long yellow dress, and large white wings.

She beckoned me to her, and I felt no fear of her. She took my hand when I reached her and silently led me back to my family's yard. I walked a few steps toward my mom, turned, and the angel was gone. It was such a short time I had been off the property that my mom did not realize I had left.

When I spoke of my glowing friends to my family, they usually said,

"You have such a vivid imagination." That's true, but these beings were real. Even as a toddler, I was sure of that. I tired of

At the time I saw my first angel, I did not know that figure was an angel. Later, when we attended a beautiful Catholic church in Frederick, Maryland, and I took catechism classes, I recognized this figure. She came to me regularly, along with other angels. They reassured me, held me, and spoke with me.

My angels became my beautiful secret for a long time. It only took me until first grade to realize that much of what I experienced was not happening for other people I knew. After that, it seemed wise to keep it to myself.

Angel Experiences

At age 12, angels stopped appearing to me as winged beings. Instead, they came in the form of large, glowing, moving lights. Each had a color or a mix of colors that distinguished them from one another. They had the same high frequency that I was accustomed to feeling before.

Frequency is the vibrational energy of a person, angel, animal or plant. Everything has a frequency, including Earth itself.

I thought that I was no longer seeing my angels and was despondent. To my mind, these were new beings who felt like angels. Eventually, they told me that they were now showing themselves to me in their natural form, which is light beings.

My angels comforted me through childhood when I felt scared and sad. They spoke words of love and encouragement, saying that I needed to be strong as I have a mission. They gave me courage, hope and strength to deal with the significant challenges in my life. My frequent conversations with my angels went on as the years passed.

It took a long time to realize that I'm meant to use my angel communicator skills to help others, and I wondered why. My angels said, "Everything has its time." For me, it took a destructive relationship to propel me toward full awareness of my gifts and mission.

While in that toxic relationship with "John", my angels began coming through more powerfully. They urged me to leave, healing me enough to keep me alive and prevent me from falling further into a Dark Night of the Soul.

It took many years for me to fully understand what my gift meant and how I can use it to help others in ways that improve their lives and propel them toward their own life purpose.

I See Angels

Many nights, I saw the varying lights that show divine protection around me. This visual sign continues today. Every night my angels come to visit me. We spend about 20 to 40 minutes conversing, having them heal me and others, and receiving information about family, friends and clients so I may help them.

They come in as oval shapes of light with movement and depth. Each angel has its particular mix of colors. Some are a roiling blend of colors, others have rays of light from the center out, and many are iridescent. Angelic light forms are gorgeous and mesmerizing. This light can grow in size, move around and immerse you within it. Most of the time, I see angels as forms of light.

Angels are all around me. They are all around you too. By the time you finish reading this book, you will have a deep understanding of what that means for you.

I'm going to share with you how I learned what my gift is. That moment was critical because it was the catalyst to getting me to where I am now. I see clients from all over the world for angelic sessions, readings, healing and spiritual counseling. This is my full time work and it is my joy. You may see a little of yourself in the next chapter.

CHAPTER TWO
I'm a Medium!

Moment of Revelation

As my health crisis continued and my relationship with "John" was ending, I had a revelation about myself. I was watching an episode of 'Long Island Medium.' It was about her childhood. She was talking about hearing her name called in the night, seeing and hearing spirits. My boyfriend at the time, John, said, "Ivory, that sounds like your childhood."

I felt and saw a golden light around me as my angels came in powerfully. It was time for me to understand the importance of one of my gifts. Having seen and spoken with angels and spirit all my life meant, "I'm a medium!"

I always wondered what an epiphany moment would feel like. Mine was breathtaking, astounding, and wonderful.

It Took So Long

That moment really was an epiphany for me. I felt floored by this realization. How could I not see it before now? I'd been seeing and hearing angels and spirit my whole life. But, as I mentioned earlier, it wasn't time for me to know I was a medium until that day. My deepest desire had long been to help people through grief via mediumship, but I had no idea I was one. There had been no sense of this at all for me.

Until this moment, I was clueless that all of my unusual experiences meant that I'm a medium. I'm not alone in this. I have had many clients who did not know about their gifts until quite late in life. I was 53 when I understood that I am a medium.

Signs

What's funny about this is that I saw spirits, talked with them, heard them, and was touched by them since very early childhood. It did not faze me to see a spirit walk through a wall, look at me and give me messages. The night after my beloved maternal grandmother, Myrtis Gill, died, she came to me in spirit form, and it eased my heart tremendously.

My angels were coming in to confirm decisions I had made that they knew would lead to happiness, success and health. They urged me to keep pursuing my lifelong passion to be a professional singer even though some people told me it was a dream, that no one could make a living doing that. My angelic team popped in at times to give me a "no" about a person I was considering letting into my life, or a dilemma I faced. There were there for me every step on my life path.

When I had ideas or inspiration about my career, family, or other areas of life, my angels came in to cover me in their high-frequency energy, confirming my thoughts as a good one.

I came to understand that my angels are available to help me with any decision, confusion, or crisis in my life. That same support is available for you too.

I'm going to share a little about my training to become a professional medium and angel communicator.

Honing Gifts

My angels told me to find a mentor for mediumship. I looked around online, and when I found the website for Susanne Wilson, the Carefree Medium, I felt a rush of energy from my angels and got a big internal "yes." It turned out that she had an office less than two miles from where I lived at that time. This was no coincidence.

Susanne took me on as a student, though she could see and feel that I was in crisis. My energy was bouncing all over the place. Her words. It was true. Mentoring to become a professional medium gave me something to look forward to, something positive despite the emotional pain I was experiencing.

It was an enjoyable endeavor which pushed out some of my previously distraught thoughts. Susanne saw all of the angels around me and immediately knew I had a special connection to them. She helped me to focus that gift into becoming an angel communicator, as well as a medium. I thought the focus of my career would be as a medium for departed humans. But, no. My angels had other plans for me. That plan was to unfold over the next two years. Often in dramatic fashion.

My year-long mentoring course with Susanne saved me. It turns out that angels had told Susanne that if she did not take me as a student, I would be lost, as in die. I believe that is true as I was feeling exhausted with life.

It was a turning point for me as the relationship with "John" went through it's final, excruciating chapter, and I was required to find the strength to get through it.

The main thing that pulled me through was my daughter, Michelle. She lost her father to suicide when she was only 15. Since then, I had been her only parent, and we are very close. There was no way I would do anything by choice to leave her without my love and support. My grandsons were another reason. I love them dearly. My mother, Wilda, called me regularly to tell me how important I am to her, dad, and the family. She encouraged me to be strong and move on with my life. My friend, Brian, called me nightly to learn how I was doing and often gave me pep talks.

There were other friends and family who supported me and kept me going through this Dark Night of the Soul. I'm not sure I could have climbed out by myself. I received so much love and light from so many people that it helped me find the light within myself again. Unfortunately, it took a village to pull me out of that hole.

Through this tie, my angels surrounded me with love, calm, peace, and whispered words of encouragement to me.

Use it For Yourself

Most people develop the ability to feel, see and hear angels solely for their personal use. Of course they desire the support, companionship, and guidance their angels can provide.

You do not need to decide how you will use these abilities now. That will unfold over time and will be clear to you when the time is right.

Let that go and read the book, do the exercises, practice, and trust. Then, if you are meant to use your abilities to help other people, your angels will guide you there, step-by-step. They will lead you, just as they do in other areas of your life.

Early in my training with Susanne, I decided I wanted to know the names of my angels. They had never told me their names, and I had not asked. So, I asked for the name of my Master Guide angel. That night I had a vivid dream about a gentle older man who radiated light and love.

This man never said a word but took my arm and helped me climb up a very steep hill. At the top, I thanked him. He looked into my eyes, and

I felt such love both from him and for him. He turned and walked away. I asked another man who that was. He replied, "That's Sir Marius."

The next day asked for a sign that Marius was my Master Guide. Less than 24 hours later, I began getting impressive signs from him. Small, white feathers were showing up in odd places like the butter section in my refrigerator, in a closed fine jewelry case unopened for years, in a secured decorative item, and on my desk. I saved all of these feathers, as they were physical confirmations from Marius.

Later, I asked Marius to leave me another while feather if he was my Master Guide. Clearly, I needed more reassurance. The following day, there were multiple balls of soft grey fluff on my patio. They were smaller than a baseball.

They were not made of fur or plant matter, and I had never seen these before, anywhere. I picked one up, and held it in my open palm. It was about three inches from my face. A breeze blew the grey fluff away, leaving a small white feather in my open palm. Chills of divine energy went through my body as I saw that proof of my Master Guide's presence in my hand. I still have that feather, as it was absolute confirmation for me.

Those balls of grey fluff appeared a few more times. They would show up long enough for me to see and watch them, then disappear shortly afterward.

Here are some ways you can use feeling, seeing and hearing angels to help yourself:

- Obtaining guidance
- Never feeling alone again
- Gaining the security of knowing your angels guard you
- Receiving intervention when you are stuck or confused

- Integrating these abilities into your current profession without announcing it

You may be guided to share your abilities with others, especially if you are an Angel Person (See Chapter 12).

If you are wondering how you can use your ability to connect with angels in a professional capacity, keep reading.

I thought my mission was to be a medium, passing on messages from deceased persons to their living loved ones. So that is what I centered my spiritual business around. But after I started doing angelic sessions, it quickly became my most popular service and remains so today.

The benefits my clients reported answered my question about the purpose of angelic readings. I have taught my methods to thousands of people with great success. However, after doing this type of session for years, it became clear that the true center of my mission is angelic communications. It is sacred work that fills me with gratitude and joy.

I could not have foreseen the number of other Angel People who would be sent to me by their angels. Part of what I do is train them to home their natural connection to angels so they may help others professionally as an angel communicator.

I know that missions evolve. It's evident in the way that I was first led to become a medium for spirit and then guided to be an angel communicator. Your angelic team can direct you to do something specific. Likely you will be passionate about doing it. At some point, your angels can guide you in a slightly, or significantly, different direction.

You will be enthusiastic about that new direction too. It's natural. This trend is much like how people tend to have a few different careers in their lifetime.

After reading the next chapter of this book, you will understand why my angels say my work is urgent.

When I finally got away from the chaos of the relationship with "John" and worked through my grief, my energy became serene. I was able to tune in to my angels even better. They began ringing angelic chimes during the night and in the early mornings. I heard a harp playing briefly, and while I own and play a harp, it was nowhere near when this occurred.

Here are a few ways in which you can use angelic communication abilities professionally:

- Being an Angel Communicator

- Writing a book about angels

- Hosting a podcast about angels

- Writing a blog about angels

- Giving presentations about angels

- Integrating your abilities into your current work

- Becoming an angel expert

The ability to communicate with angels is a spiritual gift like intuition or being an Empath. It's a God-given gift just as is given to a great athlete, a singer with perfect pitch, or having a natural aptitude for math. You can continuously develop the gifts you are both with to a higher level.

The same is true for your ability to feel, see and hear angels. No matter what your level of ability is now, you can increase your skill to the highest level possible for you.

It takes mentoring with someone, such a me, who has professional experience with angelic work. Training is done through classes, assignments, practice exercises, conducting practice readings for your family and friends, as well as people who are strangers to you.

Expect to receive kind, helpful feedback on your readings which will help you to expand your gift.

As your training proceeds, you will gain guidance on setting up your business, pitfalls to avoid, branding yourself, marketing, social media, website design, blog post writing and more.

Becoming a professional Angel Communicator requires classes for up to one year. Some courses, such as mine, provide certification, as many people seeking services do care that you have certification in what you do.

Before you begin learning how to connect with your angels, my angels would like to give you a message.

CHAPTER THREE
From My Angels to You

Connect With Your Angels

It was my angels who guided me to write this book. I felt it would help you to hear from them why it's essential to connect with your angels. So, I will let Marius, my Master Guide, and Angenis, my Guardian Angel, talk with you now.

My Angels Speak

"Many of you have long struggled with the existence of angels. You wonder if angels are genuinely watching over you, guiding you. In present times, we hear your cries asking, 'How could God let this happen?' 'Why are such terrible things happening to good people?' Understand that just as goodness and light exist, so does darkness and evil. The dark strives to hurt people, lead them to feel hopeless, and plants seeds of doubt about our existence.

You have seen a sharp increase in violence, hatred, and natural disasters. All of this has resulted in the energy of fear around the planet increasing dramatically. It is this fear that is the best weapon of darkness. You are stuck when surrounded by fear of the unknown. It is not easy to think, use your intuition, make decisions, and move forward.

Some of you think, 'I am not afraid. I am just anxious.' Know that anxiety is simply a form of fear. Recognize it for what it is so that you may address it.

It is time for you to wake up fully to our presence so that you may fully benefit from both our energy and guidance. This awakening needs to happen now to prepare humankind to clear the fear and step fully into the light. It is this that will complete the shift to enlightenment.

Imagine pushing your way through deep fog without knowing the terrain surrounding you, including the pitfalls. You could easily step off the path and into danger. However, when you can hear us and acknowledge that your angels are guiding you, it is far less likely that you will remain lost or have something negative befall you.

One of our primary purposes is to guide you toward safety; people and situations that will be helpful for you. We also lead you away from those harmful to you. When fully tuned into our presence and how we communicate with you, you find it easier to note our words and signs.

You are more likely to hear us, notice signs, and understand what you are being told. These abilities will allow you to make decisions quickly when necessary.

You can hear us and feel us. Some of you will also learn to see us. All of this will eliminate any lingering thoughts you have about us being real. Once put aside, you can begin a real relationship with your angels. We desire closeness with you, for you have been in the heart of each of your angels since the moment of your birth. That will continue throughout your lifetime.

Some of you saw your angels in childhood. You may have considered them your special friends. As a child, others may have referred to us as your invisible friends. But the truth is that you saw your angels, spoke with them, and heard their words. That ability did not disappear. Your special connection has been hidden from you, but you have the power to reveal it once again.

Until you can do these things again, we will continue to surround you with our loving energy. Being bathed in our presence will steadily raise your frequency, making it easier for you to connect with us. There is much you can do to assist with this process.

Practicing angel communication skills regularly will create a faster, deep connection with your angels. Those of you who do this will be at the front, helping others to connect as well. You are important. It is not by chance that you picked up this book. A more meaningful relationship with your angels is within your reach and part of being human.

Whether you choose to begin now with a desire to connect as soon as possible or decide to take things more slowly, there is one thing you need to know. Your entire angelic team is eagerly awaiting the moment when you can receive their communications.

An entirely different world is possible when enough of you are receiving daily guidance from your angels. With the rising frequency of each person, the frequency of your planet rises as well, bringing peace, abundance, and love for humanity.

Blessings and love to you,

Marius and Angenis (Ivory's Master Guide and Guardian Angel)

A Master Guide is one of the two angels who are with you from birth to death. They are high-level angels selected to help you stay on the path you have chosen and guide your spirit.

A Guardian Angel stays with you every second of your life. They are powerful angels who put positive thoughts into your mind and influence your will towards good.

Now we will talk about keeping a journal of your angelic experiences. Keeping a written log of your journey will be a lot of help in identifying your angels and tracking your progress.

CHAPTER FOUR
Keeping an Angel Journal

Send me the Right People

Before I moved to Sedona, once a week I was driving here to look for a house to rent. A particular professional plaza pulled my attention every time I drove past. Finally, I pulled in, parked, and noticed a "for rent" sign in a window. I peeked in the windows and heard my angels say, "This is the place." I looked at that suite eight times before I even moved to town. Remember this because it comes into play shortly.

I had moved to Sedona and was working at a big metaphysical center, doing readings and healings. From the first day, I knew I would be starting my own business eventually. It was not unusual for me to work 10 hours and see many clients in a day. Unfortunately, the excessive number of sessions led to me feeling run down and sometimes becoming ill.

During this time, I asked me angels to send me the right people to join me in my business. My request was being answered, but I was so tired that I could not see it happening.

Then I heard, "Read your journal." So, I picked it up and began reading back through the months since my move. There was a clear correlation between asking my angels for the right people to be made known to me and meeting a new spiritual friend.

Every time I made this request of my angels, I would meet someone with whom I clicked. Once I saw this I realized that I had the team necessary to start a business. I already knew where I wanted it located. That suite I mentioned earlier is precisely where we opened Sedona Soul Sisters, the metaphysical and healing center I co-own.

Had I not listened to my angels and read back in my journal, it might have taken me far longer to make the connection between my request and their response. But, instead, I heard my angels and followed their guidance and my business opened less than a year after moving to Sedona.

Why it's Helpful

I have kept spiritual journals for decades. Early into my mentoring program to become a medium, I learned which angel colors belonged to which angel. I had been seeing my angels regularly but had not consciously paid much attention to their colors.

The brilliant royal blue and purple light of my Master Guide was long familiar to me. Over time I was able to recognize a new angel coming in by seeing the same color mix repeatedly. The varying shades are something I kept track of in my journal.

Here are just a few ways keeping an angel journal will help you:

- Bonding with your angels
- Reminding you of your experiences
- Allowing you to realize the frequency of your experiences
- Refreshing your memory when needed

- Assisting you in identifying which angel is present
- Determining your peak time of day/night for angel experiences
- Tracking the messages you got and how each situation played out

I was already keeping a journal about the supernatural, paranormal, unexplained things that happened to me. So, it was natural to include the increasing angel activity, messages, and guidance in the same journal. Your angels won't mind you having a variety of information in one journal. This journal is for you, not them.

So Many Choices

Clients have asked me what type of journal they should get. There is no set answer to that. If a journal attracts you and is functional, then it's the right one for you.

Some things to consider:

- Do you like the cover design? You will be looking at it a lot
- Does it have enough pages to allow you write in it for at least a year?
- Are the lines spaced widely enough for you to write without attempting "ant writing"? Something that was very popular when I was a girl
- Are you okay with spiral bound, knowing pages will likely fall out over time?
- Is the paper easy to write on?
- Will the journal fit into your purse, bag or briefcase?

Info to Include

I'm often asked, "What kind of things should I write about?" That is also up to you. I can tell you what I include in my journal. But you are not confined to what I or anyone else does. If you are guided to write, then write. Even if it's on my list, it may not be essential to you. I am a believer in each of us being our unique selves.

The first story I ever had published was called "The Don't Be Normal Club." That short story certainly describes my feelings on the topic now, though I wrote about my teenage years. Yes, it was a real club my friend and I started in high school.

Let's dive into this. First, it will probably help if you read the list below of what I have written about in my spiritual journal. Because this book is about angels, I will limit my list to things which fit in that category.

Here goes:

- New angels coming in; their color, how they feel, any messages given

- New or important messages from my angels

- New or unusual lights, bright flashes, new colors, size changes, duration of angelic visit, location in my home or office where it was seen

- Being touched by an angel; where on the body, how it felt, and duration

- Signs from my angels

- New symbols from your angels. There are shorthand for more lengthy messages.

- Items left by my angels, such as feathers, location where they were found, what I was doing just before finding them, what I was talking about, or thinking about before discovering them.

- Celestial councils that are coming to you; their appearance, how their energy feels, and what they did or communicated to you.

- Other councils of light coming to you; their appearance, how their energy feels, what they did or communicated to you.

- Signs of angelic protection; what it looked like, how it felt, what was going on in your thoughts of life that warranted extra protection.

Format

When you make an entry in your journal, it's helpful to have some consistency. At the beginning of each entry, note the date and time of occurrence. Then, when you go back later to read your entries or verify something, you have these details and brief notes to help you keep track of what happened and when.

Then, write in detail what you experienced. Try not to eliminate anything. Those specifics can be important later.

I learned quickly in my training that the evidence is in the details. I tell my clients to give it some time if something in a reading does not make sense. Reread it later or wait for things to unfold, and it will make sense. When it comes to an angel journal, you are the client. Perhaps what you saw, heard, or felt does not make sense now. Journal the details and then put it aside for two weeks and reread it. If the meaning still eludes you, perhaps something needs to happen first. Put your entry out of your mind and allow life to unfold.

It's also possible that you received a message for someone else. It could be an immediate family member, a friend or neighbor.

The meaning of that mysterious journal entry will be understood when you are meant to understand it. I find that something will happen to make its meaning clear, such as:

- A dream
- A waking experience
- A conversation with another person
- A newscast
- An overheard conversation
- A death
- Another big life event

When something happens that is meant to trigger a memory of a message you received, you will have a sense of knowing about it. Your journal entries will help you make sense of messages in Divine time.

Getting Started

Begin by outlining what you need your angels' help with. Outline precisely the type of assistance you seek from them. Then write them a letter. Write from the heart, being open and honest. Writing this letter to your angels can be so healing for you.

Take some time to get quiet and listen to your angels' messages in response to your letter. Then write down the angelic messages you received. Include opportunities that opened for you, people who came into your life, and other instances related to your request.

I've been keeping journals for most of my adult life. They are an excellent way to remember important angelic events and see how much you have grown in your spiritual life.

My journals cover the last 40 years. I reviewed them for parts of this book to ensure that my memory was correct. It was not always on target, forgetting some details. Few can rely solely on their memory. Any detective will tell you that ten people can go through the same experience together, and each person will have a different story to tell. That is because we tend to focus on small parts of an experience.

The same is true for you with your angelic events. Perhaps you will want to write a book of your own in the future. Again, having detailed notes about what happened will make it easier and more accurate.

How often do you need to write? You only need to make entries in your journal as you feel compelled to do so. When something spectacular or new happens, you will be excited. Your fingers will fly over the keyboard. By the way, feel free to keep your journal online. Don't let an aversion to handwriting stop you from keeping a log of your angelic memories.

I don't write every day. Days or weeks may go by with no new entries. Then there are times that I write a few times a day. That's how angelic activity goes. Sometimes it feels like a welcoming heavy rain on parched land. Finally, something happens and you have a reason to journal again. At times you will be kept hopping, trying to log everything you experience.

As I said, there are times when nothing is happening. For me, those times are when nothing new is going on. I don't log every time that my Master Guide or Guardian Angel visit me because it happens every night. We are also conversing through the days, but that's a regular thing, so I don't log it. Not unless they say or do something that feels momentous.

Improving Spiritual Gifts

Any time you consciously work on a spiritual skill, such as communicating with angels, you also improve your other gifts. The main one that people report increasing is their intuitive ability. All these gifts are given to us by God.

You and every person on this planet can see, feel, or hear their own angels. They can develop their intuitive ability to the highest degree possible for them at the time. These gifts will be beneficial to you in your personal and business life, as well as bonding with your angels.

Why does tuning into your angels increase other spiritual gifts? Because you likely have barriers within you that are currently preventing you from experiencing there things. Reading this book tells your angels that you are ready to bring those walls down.

Get Out of Your Own Way

How did those barriers get there? It can be consciously or unconsciously. Perhaps you were raised around someone who felt anything unexplained was wrong or evil. Maybe you grew up in a religion that looked negatively upon spiritual gifts. Society, in general, can push those abilities down so that you forget you ever had them. But they are there, waiting to be encouraged to blossom. It's never too late.

Where to begin? So easy. Get your journal as soon as possible. Then, come back to this page and start reading again.

You have your journal; now it's time to record your activities. First, write today's date and the time. Then, in your own words, write, "Today, I begin my journey of getting to know my angels. I permit myself to drop all barriers, known and unknown. I am ready to move forward and have a deep, meaningful relationship with my angels."

Woohoo! You did it! Putting that in writing creates an energetic shift. Your journey has truly begun. Maybe you already feel a little different inside. Imagine how you will feel once you complete reading the upcoming chapters and doing the exercises in them.

The next night, write this in your own words, "I drop any remaining barriers that prevent me from seeing, hearing and feeling my angels. I welcome my angels and ask to receive clear signs from them." Read this out loud every night after turn out the lights in your bedroom. You need to be in bed, relaxed, and ready to communicate with your angels when you say this.

After I do my nighttime prayers and protection, I do distance healing on those I know need it or have asked for it. Then I say this simple statement, "Angels surround me. Angels protect me." Then I lie still and relaxed, looking toward a dark area of my bedroom. I'm ready to see my angels, feel their wondrous energy and hear their loving words for me.

It is easiest to experience your angels when your mind is quiet, without distractions.

You have received the underlying information you need to begin delving into the process of angel communications. This work will require regular practice to gain and strengthen the abilities you seek.

It's time to start learning how to feel your angels. I like to begin with this because feeling your angels touch tends to be a powerful experience. It's also usually the easiest skill to obtain. Let's find out what you feel when your angels touch you.

CHAPTER FIVE
Feeling Your Angels

I Just Killed Them All

My family moved to Prescott, Arizona in the mid-'70's when I was in my junior year of high school. While my parents were on vacation, I borrowed my dad's truck, which had had told me not to do. See, I'm not perfect. I loaded my siblings, Allen, Ruth, and Mary, into the open bed. My sister, Dee, my boyfriend and his brother were in the cab with me. Then, we followed another vehicle to a party in Government Canyon, located in the hills outside of town.

I was nervous about driving so fast on winding dirt roads, with steep drop-offs and no guard rails. But I was 16, and my judgment was flawed. The car ahead sped up, and I followed suit. I remember worrying that I would lose sight of them and not be able to find the party. Then we came to a sharp left turn. The truck began to slide. Suddenly, the front and rear right-side tires of the truck were off the road.

My thought was, "Oh my God. I just killed them all." Silently, I prayed to God and asked my angels to intervene. Immediately I felt an immense surge of angelic energy around us and the vehicle. That energy left me breathless, covered in hard chills. I felt like we were in a protective bubble of calm. Miraculously, the truck never tipped to the right. There is no logical explanation for this.

Very quickly, we were guided to the left and the truck rocketed up a steep dirt road that happened to be at that particular place. Interestingly, I did not see that road, but my angels did. The incline slowed the truck, and we came to a hard stop against a rock.

I knew our angels had lifted the truck and saved all of us. As I sat there in shock, shaking, I was thanking my angels and God for intervening and saving our lives. The angelic energy remained around us until I was calm enough to drive. Their peaceful energy soothed me, as they whispered words of love because they knew that I felt terrible. Then, as I settled, I felt the angels' gradually leave the cab of the truck until all that remained with us were my two primary angels.

That powerful lesson led to an aversion to speeding or driving faster than conditions warrant. I am not a party pooper, I'm simply a woman who knows how badly that situation could have ended. When my angels tell me to slow down, stop, or take a different route, I do it.

Yes, my parents did find out about that adventure. I confessed it to them when I was in my 30's. They were shocked at the near tragedy, but it turns out that they knew I had driven dad's truck. It had a tell-tale crack on the bug shield, thanks to the big rock it ran into.

The face that a crack was the only damage is stunning. I needed my parents to know the truth about that incident. Not only because of my guilt weighing on my conscious but because of how angels saved us all from serious injury or event death.

I'm not sure they believed me about the angelic intervention, but they have come to have much more open minds about such things. I understand how it can be challenging to believe, or even imagine, something you have never experienced yourself. But that is one of the gifts of connecting with your angels. You will have incredible moments of your own.

Surprising Sensation

I'm going to start by helping you to feel the touch and presence of your angels. Through my client sessions, it has been apparent that feeling the touch of an angel is a profound experience. Knowing that the angel touching you is your angel enhances this powerful encounter.

Angels have a frequency, just as we humans do. The difference is that angelic frequency is much higher than ours. The higher the frequency, the stronger the sensation you will receive.

Archangels have an even higher frequency than angels do. I will walk you through some exercises to help you learn how to feel angels and Archangels. When you understand what different angel frequencies feel like, you can identify who is touching you or near you.

Use Your Senses

The meaning of that mysterious journal entry will be understood when you are meant to understand it. I find that something will happen to make its meaning clear, such as:

- A dream
- A waking experience
- A conversation with another person
- A newscast
- An overheard conversation
- A death
- Another big life event

When something happens that is meant to trigger a memory of a message you received, you will have a sense of knowing about it. Your journal entries will help you make sense of messages in Divine time.

The least common sensation is feeling a strong sense of presence. However, I have noted that this reaction is happening more often of late. My angels say this is due to the Celestial realms lowering our internal barriers. This lowering is one of the reasons my angels wanted me to write this book now. They want this how-to information available to anyone who desires it.

Let's Get Ready

Before you attempt these exercises, set aside at least 10 minutes to be in a quiet place. Minimal distractions is essential. A calm environment will assist you in having success as soon as possible.

Some will be able to feel their angel's energy right away. There are those I call Angel People who are born with a special connection to angels.

For most, it takes time and patience. Gaining these skills is not a race. I gently remind you that obtaining these abilities cannot be forced. You are far more likely to feel, see and hear your angels when you practice regularly. But you cannot move up the timeline. Understand that everything happens in its own time.

Stay relaxed and trust that your angels guided you to this book. They are not going to drop the ball now. Your angelic team will guide you through gaining these abilities every step of the way. If you find yourself getting tense or frustrated, take a break.

Close your eyes, take deep breaths in through your nose and let each breath out slowly through your mouth.

When you are calm, say out loud, "Angels, I trust you to guide me. I trust that I will gain this skill in Divine time." Divine time means that something will happen at the time it is supposed to. Therefore, you cannot rush it.

Feeling Your Master Guide

Have your journal and something to write with at hand. You will be making notes. Sit in a comfortable chair. Put both feet flat on the floor.

Make sure your arms are uncrossed and resting on the arms of a chair or on your lap. Then, do the calming breathing outlined above for 5 to 10 breaths. All of this clears your energy and makes you a better channel for receiving the sensation of your angel's touch.

Now, put your focus on your left shoulder and upper arm. Out loud, ask that all your angels and guides move back and ask that only your Master Guide stand at your left side. Ask your Master Guide, who is an angel, to touch you on that part of your body. Remain relaxed and focused on your left shoulder and upper arm for a minute, or so.

If you do not feel any change, ask your Master Guide to increase their energy so you can feel them. Again, stay relaxed and focused. Give this process a few minutes this time.

Repeat this cycle a few times for a total of no more than 10 minutes. After that, you are trying too hard. However, you are making progress with this, even if you do not yet feel it.

Write the date, time and "Feeling My Angels-Exercise 1" in your journal. Detail what you experienced during this exercise, even if you felt nothing.

I recommend practicing this daily if possible. However, if you are becoming tense or stressing about it, you will likely find it helpful to take a break for a couple of days.

Being tense changes your frequency and makes it more difficult to experience anything. It's the Celestial version of getting in your own way.

When this happens, it's better to put your attention and energy into other things; preferably things you enjoy. I have found that putting my energy into something positive that moves me forward, personally or professionally, releases stress and other frequency lowering emotions.

Come back to this exercise when you feel clear and serene again. Please do not go to Exercise 2 until you have had at least three successes with Exercise 1. You need to feel confident in your ability to feel your angels and know that you are not fantasizing. That's another internal barrier that drops with practice of these exercises. If you have not been successful with Exercise 1 within two weeks, reference the Troubleshooting chapter of this book.

Continue to make entries in your journal with each practice session. Keeping track of these sessions will allow you to see your progress more clearly, which is both reassuring and motivating.

Know that you will have the same sensation with every angel that touches you or is nearby. The difference is the intensity. It is just one of the ways to identify which angels is with you.

As you move forward with your abilities and learn how to see your angels, the combination of feeling and seeing them makes it easy to know the identify of the angel.

Feeling an Archangel

The focus of this book is on helping you to develop a close relationship with your angels. Archangels are not attached to any one person. They are available for everyone and can be with many people at once.

Some people have a special attachment to a specific Archangel, but that is not the same as having them as part of your angelic team.

I include this exercise so you can feel the difference between the frequency of an angel and that of an Archangel. Every angel has a frequency. You will eventually note how high the frequency is of an angel that touches you or is nearby.

Only angels with exceptionally high frequency can be your Master Guide or Guardian Angel. Yet, the frequency of an Archangel is higher. So, prepare yourself for a powerful experience. When I feel an Archangel's presence, I get intense chills head to toe that they actually hurt and my breath is take away momentarily.

Have your journal and writing implement at hand again. Just as you did with the previous exercise, you will be making notes.

Sit in a comfortable chair. Put both feel flat on the floor. Have your arms uncrossed and resting on the chair arms or your lap. Do the calming breathing for five to ten breaths.

Now, put your awareness on your left shoulder and upper arm. Out loud, ask Archangel Raphael to touch you on that part of your body. Remain relaxed and focused on your left shoulder and upper arm for about a minute.

If you do not feel any change, ask Archangel Raphael to increase his energy so you can feel it. Again, stay relaxed and focused. Give this exercise a few minutes this time.

Repeat this cycle a few times for no more than a total of ten minutes. Again, if you are becoming tense, take a break. I assure you that you cannot push through to success in this endeavor. Like other angel communication skills, feeling your angels is a skill you cannot force.

Make a note in your journal of the date, time and details of what you felt each time you attempted this exercise. If you did not feel anything, note your emotions as well. At the end of this chapter, I will give you lists of emotions that will block you as well as those that will help you open.

Remember, you are learning a new skill that can be life-changing for you. It's okay if you are not able to do these things right away. Practice regularly and stay relaxed. Tensing up about it will make it more difficult for you to connect to your angels.

Feeling the touch of an angel sometimes does happen quickly with students who are new to all of this. They close their eyes, tune in to their left shoulder and upper arm and instantly feel a strong sensation. But that's not true for everyone.

Be easy on yourself. Give yourself time to open to this. Keep your energy clear and receptive. You will feel the touch of an angel when you are meant to, and no sooner.

Feeling Other Angels on Your Team

The purpose of this exercise is to allow you to feel the touch, frequency, of some of your other angels. Remember, you have a whole team of angels and guides with you.

I recommend starting with asking your Guardian Angel, your other primary angel, to stand at your left side. Tune in to feeling their frequency a few times.

Again, have your journal and writing implement, or laptop, at hand. You will be making notes and, by now, you likely understand the value of them from previous practice sessions.

Sit in a comfortable chair. Put both feet flat on the floor. Have your arms uncrossed and resting on the chair arms or your lap. Do the calming breathing for five to ten breaths.

All of this clears your energy and makes you a better channel for receiving the sensation of your angel's touch.

Now, put your awareness on your left shoulder and upper arm. Out loud, ask that all your angels and guides move back and allow just your Guardian Angel, or another angel if you wish, to stand to your left. Ask that angel to touch you on that part of your body. Remain relaxed and focused on your left shoulder and upper arm for about a minute.

If you do not feel any change, ask your angel to please increase their energy so that you can feel them. Then, again, stay relaxed and focused. Give this exercise a few minutes this time.

Repeat this cycle a few times until you are confident that you feel the same sensation at the same intensity each time.

The other change I have noted is that when one of my angels appears, the frequency rises around me. I feel this as a vibration in the air. The more high-level the angel is, the higher the vibration.

Make a note in your journal of the date, time, the angel you invited to touch you, and what you felt. Remember to note any emotions you were experiencing if this session is unsuccessful so you can avoid that emotion next time.

If this is happening for you, before you practice again, read the "Troubleshooting" chapter of this book for specific methods to raise your frequency and overcome your barriers.

There is a momentous experience tied to this that is an indication of your frequency rising dramatically. In the "Troubleshooting" chapter, you will also learn the signs that your frequency is increasing.

When you have confidence in your ability to feel the touch of your angels, you are ready to move on to another exciting skill: seeing your angels.

Emotions Rule

Your ability to feel, see and hear your angels can be significantly affected by your emotions. Therefore, it's essential to be aware of this before practicing the exercises in this book. This will help you start with the best possible chance of success.

You are likely to discover a pattern as to which emotion(s) are most blocking for you. The emotions listed below will block your receptive ability:

- Fear
- Anxiety
- Doubt
- Anger
- Jealousy
- Envy

Let's talk about jealousy and envy for a moment. These nasty emotions can be so detrimental to your journey. Mostly that happens when we compare ourselves to someone else. Wishing you had felt your angels right away is one example of stepping into a danger zone.

On the other hand, some emotions are super high-frequency, making you a more open channel for angelic communications. They are:

- Gratitude
- Excitement
- Joy
- Love
- Peace
- Forgiveness

Try to keep yourself in one or more of these positive emotions, and you will be like a well-tuned radio. You'll be able to pick up frequencies and messages much more clearly.

No matter what your frequency is now, your angels are with you. They do not abandon or reject you when you feel low or are experiencing a character flaw. Instead, your angels are on your side for life, supporting and guiding you to rise above.

Once you can hear your angels, it's time to learn how to see them. The next chapter will guide you through that and prepare you for the glorious visions your angels present.

CHAPTER SIX
Seeing Your Angels

What's Up With the Lights?

As I mentioned earlier, when I was a young girl, my angels would come in as winged beings with beautiful faces, long flowing hair, and robes. I'm not sure if that was because I was raised as a Catholic and had seen paintings and statues of angels in the Bible and in the Cathedral we attended.

My encounters with traditional angelic forms continued until I was 12 or 13. At this time, they began coming to me as forms of light.

At first, I was not sure what was happening. These other-worldly-looking lights had the feeling of angels, but I was confused. Not only was I pre-pubescent, dealing with hormones racing through my body, but I was struggling with some frightening paranormal events and emotional damage from abuse by a neighbor a few years earlier.

I was a quiet, private girl outside of my home. For whatever reason, I did not ask for help from anyone. Truthfully, I did not talk about my angels much and dealt with my encounters myself.

In my junior high years, I felt rather abandoned. I thought I had lost my ability to see angels. Once I understood, "Hey, these are my angels," I was right back on track with my connection with them. My angels found this time amusing. Angels do have a sense of humor, which they have needed with me. I have not always been an easy person to guide. We'll get into that later. Oh boy!

My angels told me that in the Celestial plane, they are beings of light. I was now seeing them in their actual state. They were so lovely, with a vast array of colors, design and often iridescence.

What Angels Look Like

For me, when an angel appears, it most often comes in as a medium ball of colored light. It begins as a sideways oval around 2 feet long and a foot high. Then it grows larger.

My Master Guide used to come into whatever room I was sleeping in and grow to the size of an entire wall. Two years ago, he began doing something different. He comes in, then expands to about 5 feet long and 4 feet high, and slowly floats around the room. But he remains in my field of vision. Sometimes he appears on the pillow next to mine. Because he is so close, I feel his frequency more powerfully. When my Master Guide does this, I feel wrapped in love.

My angels stay between 10 and forty minutes, on average. You will learn that I enjoy scientific experiments. That is true with my angels too. Luckily, they like them and fully participate.

Angels can surround you in their light, which is a euphoric experience. You find yourself encased in your angel's light and energy. This intensity is rare but worth the wait.

Angels appear in other forms as well. Here are the primary ways they appear:

- Sparks of white or gold light. These are bright pinpoints of light that flash briefly. You are most likely to see them first in your peripheral vision. When you do, say "Hello angel!" Acknowledging your angel lets them know that you understand what you are seeing and are receptive to seeing more. Eventually, you will see these lights straight ahead of you and even close-up.

- Tiny comets of white or gold light. These are bright pinpoints of light that appear and travel across the room in an arc or straight line. They look remarkably like a tiny comet indoors. As stated above, greet your angel, so they know you welcome seeing them again.

- Soft balls of white or gold light. These can be between the size of a baseball and a softball-sized light which is soft with a hazy edge. It may appear and then disappear. It can also travel around the room. Greet your angel with joy.

- Bright balls of white or gold light. These are the same size as the balls described above, but the light is bright, and the edges are more distinct. I have seen them pop in and out quickly or move across or around the room rapidly.

- For me, they sometimes pop up large and bright between my face and the book I'm reading. Well, hello!

- Protective light. I go into detail about this in Chapter 12-Going Rogue.

Now I'm going to teach you how to see your angels.

How to See Your Angels

The easiest way to see your angels is in a dark room. I do this nightly before I go to sleep. Being relaxed in my bed with no distractions works best for me. You will likely benefit from this as well.

Before you begin, say out loud, "I ask my angels and guides to move back and allow only my Master Guide to come forward at this time and stand at my side."

Lie down, keep your eyes open and focus on a specific, dark area in your room. Then allow your vision to relax, almost to the point where your eyes cross. Doing this will enable you to see with your third eye.

Remember those pictures that looked like many dots, but when you relax your vision, a 3D image pops out? It is very much like that.

You will be seeing your angels with your third eye. I know this because I am very nearsighted and cannot see clearly beyond three feet away without my glasses. But I can see angels and other beings 18 to 20 feet away by letting my third eye do the seeing.

Relax your body by breathing calmly in through your nose and out through your mouth. Measured breathing will help you be as receptive as possible to the experience.

Give this exercise five to ten minutes. After that, it will be like pulling teeth, and that's no good.

As your focus relaxes, you may see a ball of colored light appear. It is natural to want to get a good look at this phenomenon. People will sit up in bed, focus their vision, and poof; the light is gone. They are trying to see their angel with their eyes instead of their third eye.

If this happens to you, relax your vision again. Your angel will be right there again. As exciting as this is, make an effort to stay calm. Keeping your energy serene makes you a better channel to receive these celestial visions.

Make a mental note of the size, colors, and frequency or vibration that you experience as you see your Master Guide. You are a spiritual scientist at this moment. You will want to jot this information down in your journal after your Master Guide leaves for the night, or you grow too tired to keep watching. I often watch and communicate until I fall asleep.

Seeing Your Master Guide

You need to develop a close relationship with this angel as they are the head of your angelic team and one of your angels.

Follow the steps outlined above under "How to See Your Angels." The light of your Master Guide is going to be bright and powerful. Remember, this is a high-level angel you are seeing.

After you have seen your Master Guide and they have gone, thank your Master Guide for the gift of seeing their beautiful light. Let them know how much seeing them means to you and that you are open to seeing them nightly. You can say this out loud or in your head if you are concerned with waking someone else.

There is no need to release your Master Guide as they are with you all the time.

Remember to note the date, time, what you saw, felt, and anything else you think is essential. These journal notations will help identify which angel you observe as you know more about your angelic team.

When you see your angel, they are also communicating with you. You may hear them or have an innate knowing that you are receiving information. Either way, your Higher Self will receive the information. That means that you get the benefits of what they say, even if you are not consciously aware of receiving it.

Seeing Your Guardian Angel

It's a good idea to learn what your other primary angel looks like since every angel has its unique blend of colors. That is your Guardian Angel. This angel is with you every second of your life, just as your Master Guide is.

Why can't you see your angels all the time? Because humans have a lot of distractions. Even light is a form of interference when you are looking for your angels. It is much easier to see them when you are wholly focused on the task and in a dark room.

Let's find out what your Guardian Angel's colors are. I do not recommend doing this the same night you look for your Master Guide. Until you can see your angels easily, you need a break of at least one day between practice sessions.

Before you begin, say out loud, "I ask my angels and guides to move back and allow only my Guardian Angel to come forward at this time and stand at my side."

Lie down, keep your eyes open and focus on a specific, dark area in your room. Then allow your vision to relax, almost to the point where your eyes cross. Doing this will enable you to see with your third eye.

Relax your body by breathing calmly in through your nose and out through your mouth. Measured breathing will help you be as receptive as possible to the experience.

Give this exercise five to ten minutes. Again, make a mental note of what you saw, heard, and anything else that seems important to you. Remember to note the date, time first. You may end up with decades worth of journals and experiences. It makes it so easy to remember when things happened, no matter how long ago it was.

Out loud, thank your Guardian Angel for help you to see their beautiful light. Let them know how much it means to you and that you are open to seeing them nightly.

There is no need to release them as they are with you all the time.

If you try for 5 minutes and don't see them, it's not going to happen this time. Wait till the next night to try again. One angel per night, for your sake. This type of intense focus is tiring. Plus, it puts undue pressure on you. It's best to practice a bit every night you can. When it's the right time to experience it, you will see angels.

I would love to hear from you when you see one of your angels for the first time. It's nearly as exciting for me as it is for you. Your angels will be celebrating your success, and so will I.

Please do not move on to other angels until you can see your Master Guide and Guardian Angel easily and regularly. You are gaining that deep knowledge that angels exist and are with you. This insight is important in being able to receive the most angelic guidance possible.

Seeing Other Angels on Your Team

Now that you have mastered the ability to see your Master Guide and Guardian Angel, it's time to find out how your other angels appear. These can include your Protection Guide, Teacher Guide, Medical Guide, and others.

They have specific purposes for being assigned to your team at this time. When you know why they are with you, it helps you focus on that issue and work through it faster.

Before you begin, say out loud, "I ask that my angels and guides move back and allow one other angel or guide to come forward at this time."

Guides are additional members of your angelic team called in to assist you by your two primary angels. They are with you for a specific purpose as long as you need them. They may be angels, the spirit of a deceased person known or unknown to you, or another high-level being.

Just as you did with the earlier exercises, lie down, keep your eyes open and focus on a specific, dark area in your room.

Then allow your vision to relax, almost to the point where your eyes cross. Softening your eyes will enable you to see with your third eye.

To relax, breathe calmly in through your nose and out through your mouth. Doing this will unwind your body and help you be as receptive as possible to the experience. Give this exercise five to ten minutes.

Again, make a mental note of what you saw, heard, and anything else you want to record. Remember to note the date, time first.

The Big Dream

I was still unhappy in my relationship. I had resolved my health issue, but I could feel my boyfriend, "John", pulling away from me emotionally. His addiction had escalated dramatically. I found myself torn between leaving and trying harder to help him. Yes, it was the usual Lightworker tendency to put others before me. I've come a long way with that since then.

Every day and night, I asked my angels to give me a clear sign of what I needed to do. For four months, I waited for their response. I knew it would come, but I was anxious to receive it. My mind was saying "go," but my heart was reluctant.

One night, I had a vivid dream that I was sitting up in my bed. All my angels were around me. A few sat on the bed next to me; others knelt on the floor at the bedside. They were holding me, stroking my head, soothing me. I was so happy to have all of them with me. There was a warm golden glow around us. Their energy was incredibly loving, and I felt a sense of wonder. My Master Guide, Marius, said, "You have to leave him to save yourself." I woke up crying.

I knew Marius was right. Staying in that relationship was damaging to me, and "John" was not improving his behavior. It was getting much worse. That dream was precisely the kick in the pants I needed to wake me up to reality. I needed to see the truth, face it, and move forward with my life.

This wake-up call from my angels helped me begin to let go emotionally, plan for the next chapter of my life, finish my mediumship studies and move to Sedona. Without this intervention, I don't believe I would be where I am, helping people in the way I'm doing.

Take Your Time

I recommend that you give yourself two to four weeks to develop your ability to see your angels before moving on to the next chapter. Becoming successful at seeing your angels can take some time. It depends on your skill level and the barriers you have within.

After four weeks, it is best to move to the next chapter and come back to this one later. Some people can see angels right away. Others can hear them but not see them. Over time, most people can do all three: feel, see and hear their angels.

Find the skill you are best at and work on that to build your confidence. Then go about getting the other skills down, but at your own time. When the time is right, you will see angels. It will likely surprise you. I get excited emails from clients who just saw, felt, or heard their angels for the first time. I love hearing from them.

Stay relaxed and let your abilities unfold in their own time.

Let's move on to the ability to hear your angels. You begin the process of receiving messages from your angels more clearly and frequently when this next skill is gained. It's exhilarating so let's start.

CHAPTER SEVEN
Hearing Your Angels

Plenty of Toilet Paper

In the Fall of 2018, my angels began telling me to stock up on certain products. They urged me to get another package of toilet paper, a few more canned goods. I was curious as to why, but I know better than to ignore the guidance of my angels.

Every time I went to the grocery store, I heard "get some dried goods." They even told me to purchase large cans of dehydrated foods, which I did. I felt a little goofy buying these items when I had no idea why I need them. But I pushed past that emotion. This push to get dry goods went on for over a year, and I had a sufficient supply of extra food and water on hand. Due to their directives, I had also bought some propane canisters, a manual can opener, and a water purifying system.

I dutifully got what they wanted me to get. My kitchen pantry filled up. I turned to a linen closet to handle the overflow jugs of water and more. It seemed a bit much, having so much on hand, but I mostly put it out of my mind. Luckily, I did not need to resort to lining my garage with shelves for the overflow. That would have looked a bit strange to my neighbors.

My business partner, Rozlyn, was having the same thing happen. During this same period, her angels were telling her to buy the same items. When we realized we were both receiving these messages, we laughed a bit but agreed it was wise to follow our angels' guidance. We at Sedona Soul Sisters felt that something big was coming, and it did not feel good. These angelic messages added to our sense of trouble on the horizon.

I told my family and some friends what I had been instructed to do by my angels. Some of them thanked me and stocked up. Others politely listened and did not buy anything. A few laughed a bit. I knew some of them would not take it seriously, but I felt I had to give them a heads-up. I did not want them to be caught short. Most of the clients I passed this on to did stock up. Just another example of 'Only in his home town, among his relatives and in his own house is a prophet without honour' (Mark 6:1-6). Let's face it; our relatives tend to see us as we were, not as we are. It was an issue thousands of years ago. People are going to do what they want to do.

Then Covid 19 hit. People panicked and quickly store shelves were empty of nonperishable products, water, and toilet paper. Heck, finding toilet paper required a veritable treasure hunt. I felt reasonably serene about it because I knew I had what I needed to get by for a while. I was able to share supplies with people who could not find what they needed. That felt good.

The day I heard about the scarcity of items in grocery stores and how people were buying up everything they could find; I sat down and thanked my angels profusely. I was, and am, so grateful to them for watching over me and ensuring I was okay. Living alone has been a bit daunting during this unstable time, but I was thankful for not having to go on county-wide searches for toilet paper.

This situation sounds funny now, but it sure wasn't at the time. I know that this experience opened some of my family and friend's eyes to the validity of angels and the value of hearing them.

Our angels know the truth of a situation. Despite what we want to believe or how hard we try to ignore reality; our angels will clarify when we are ready to face it. Then we need to be prepared to act based on their words.

It's helpful to know what to listen for, so you can pick up on as many angelic messages as possible. It reduces the likelihood that you will dismiss them as a weird thought. Let's move into the specifics of hearing your angel's words.

One way that angels can send you messages is through a third party. They may have a family member or friend pass a message on to you. This type of angel communication can also happen through synchronicities such as repeatedly seeing a specific person, book title, course name, etc.

Another way your angels may communicate with you is through your intuition. You may have a sudden understanding of a complex issue, receive an inspiring thought, have a gut instinct, see images in your mind, have dreams that later come true, or have words hover in your mind. Those are messages from straight from your angel to you. Direct communication is a more intimate exchange between you and your angels.

You can ask your angels to send you direct messages. Then it would help if you looked for them, so they don't slip by unnoticed. Understand that the more often you ask for information from your angels and act on their guidance, the more messages you will receive.

It helps you to live at your full potential when you receive intuitive guidance. You don't need to rely on the opinion or direction of others, except in extreme situations where you cannot trust your intuition. Listening to words from your angels is a beautiful way to help build your self-confidence. This practice is helpful to you with life in general, not only concerning your relationship with your angels.

Where Did That Come From?

Your angels talk to you often. You will hear angels as a thought in your head. This dilemma leads to my clients asking, "How do I know the difference between my thoughts and angelic messages?" Good question. The first time a client asked it, I launched another of my beloved scientific investigations. I spent many hours tuning into the specifics of angelic messages to give the details to my clients. I made notes and looked at the information gathered. The resulting particulars helped them catch more of their angel's messages.

I discovered that messages from your angels are most often out of context from your thoughts or activity. You are likely to think, "Why am I thinking about that now?" or "Where did that come from?" This questioning is because it's not your thought. Your angels are attempting to get your attention and guide you to do something meaningful on your behalf.

You could be writing a grocery shopping list, and you hear, "Why aren't you working on that book?" I have heard that message many times. I was not thinking about my book, writing, or angels in general. This deviation from my thinking was an intrusive, odd thought. Lucky for me, I knew it was a heads up. Hey, Ivory, your angels want to talk with you!

So Annoying!

Don't worry. Angels laugh when I say that. They know it's true. Messages from your angelic team are not always welcome. You might be sick, depressed, going through chaos, in the middle of moving, or facing divorce. Let me give you an example of that.

When the second round of "You need to host a talk show. You need to write a book" happened, I was neck-deep with remodeling my new home, packing up my current house, and trying to find time between all of that to see clients. It was not a great time to begin writing this book. My angels did not get that. Again, they have never been human, so they don't understand being overwhelmed, sick, depressed, exhausted, and the other aspects of being human that get in the way of our spiritual goals.

I did what I do naturally; I communicated with them. I explained that circumstances made it impossible for me to begin writing at that time. They kept talking to me about the book. They are tenacious, but so am I. Life would not allow me to do as they asked at that time. I repeatedly let them know that I would host a talk show and write the book but could not do it yet. Over a few months, that message from them began to lessen. Receiving fewer pushes to write and host a show was a relief as I had plenty on my plate. The last thing I needed then was more messages about big projects I was not prepared to begin.

You will likely need to explain similar situations to your angels. They will keep talking to you about whatever they want you to do, but eventually, they will ease up a bit. I think it's good they don't stop entirely, as I appreciate a slight push on projects. If your angels feel something is essential, it is!

Here is another good reason to keep your angel journal at hand. Be sure to make a note of what your angels say. When you have more time to focus, pull out your journal and remind yourself of what they want you to do.

Remember to list the date, time, and exactly what you heard. Your angels will know you are doing this, and it seems to help them believe that you noted the message and plan to act on it.

Qualities to Expect

More than one angel can speak to you at the same time. Sometimes they communicate as a collective voice. They are helpful, encouraging, loving, and calm. You can find them annoying when you cannot follow them, and the same message keeps flowing in.

They can be funny. Angels have a sense of humor. Good thing, too, since they are dealing with humans, and it must be worse than herding cats.

You may hear them as a whisper, a normal voice, or a loud declaration. When you hear them, it is not in a separate voice. If you are a natural medium, you may rarely hear angels talk with your ears.

You can have resistance to following their guidance. Angels may say, "Tell your waiter that his angels are giving him extra protection." Perhaps you are not comfortable passing on such messages, and your waiter doesn't look particularly welcoming. Been there, experienced that!

They may guide you to do something you would never choose to do on your own. These situations can include going into a career you never considered, going out with someone who is not your type, stop going out with someone you are deeply in love with or taking a class you don't understand why you would need.

Ringing Ears

Ringing ears are not always a medical issue. When my angels come in, my left ear begins to ring at a very high pitch. It stays that way until my angels start talking to me. I call my left ear my angel ear. My friends have this too, but not always the left ear. So, if one of your ears begins to ring and the pitch is so high it can turn into a squeal, know that your angels are asking you to pay attention.

What does this ringing mean for you? That depends. Here are some reasons you may hear this angelic frequency ringing:

- They want you to know they are with you.

- You are engaging in an activity damaging to your frequency, such as watching a scary movie, looking at violent news stories, or having a negative conversation.
- They have a message for you.
- Your attention is being drawn to something specific.

It's difficult to hear what your angels have to say to you if you are not paying attention, distracted by tv or music, or not setting aside time for meditation or reflection. Quiet time is necessary for you to hear them clearly, so you get the entire message.

When you hear that sudden high-pitched ringing in one ear, eliminate any distractions you can; start by turning off the television or music, hang up the phone, go to a quiet space. Let your angels know that you understand they want to communicate something to you. Tune in and listen as you breathe slowly and deeply.

If you cannot hear them, you can ask questions to narrow down to yes or no questions.

When you hit on the right question, your angels are likely to give you a rush of angelic energy. You will feel it the way you identified how you felt it in the chapter on Feeling Your Angels.

Ask things like, "Is this movie not in my best and highest good?", "Are these people damaging to my frequency?", "Do I need to eliminate news from my life for a while?" You will eventually ask a question that gets you a response in the form of divine energy.

Often you will know what your angels want to bring up with you. Your intuition, or common sense, will tell you. After all, you know the emotions that lift you and those that pull you down.

That does not mean you will be perfect and do everything you are supposed to. Change takes time. If you are motivated to raise your frequency and have a close relationship with your angels, that will help you make the changes necessary for you.

If you have repeated ringing in both ears, it would be wise to see a doctor. Not every ringing is spiritual. If your hearing is good, messages from your angels are likely the explanation for your ringing ear.

Now I'll share with you how angels use music to communicate with you.

Music

For some people, the first sign they receive from their angels was hearing angelic music or singing, which originated outside of the material world.

Here are some of the ways you may hear these signs:

- Chimes
- Harp music
- Beautiful singing

The chimes can sound as one tone, a few, or a little melody. You may hear the same few musical notes again and again. They can happen when you are sleeping, in the twilight between waking and sleeping or between sleeping and waking, and even when you are fully awake. There will be no explanation for the chimes. You don't have anything like that in the room, perhaps not even in the home. If you search for the source, you won't find it.

When you hear harp music, it can be a strum across every string on a harp, plucking a few strings or a melody. Again, there will not be a source for this sound. Though I do have a harp, I store it in a room on the far side of my home. Yet, I will hear harp music in my bedroom when no one else is in the house. The resonance of the notes lingers in the air. You can feel them. So even if you hear a harp playing while you sleep, you can feel the notes lingering in the air when you wake.

Another way your angels may choose to communicate with you is through songs you hear. It will be a song that means something to you or answers a question, for perhaps it is a song you have always loved and have not heard for a long time. That alone catches your attention. Then you tune into the lyrics and realize you are getting a message in response to a situation.

It can also be hearing a song repeatedly in a relatively short period. Again, the lyrics will mean something to you specifically. You may also note a series of songs that share a similar theme.

You can receive this type of sign by having a song start playing in your mind, asking your angels for an indication regarding a specific issue, having the lyrics answer your question or a song playing which cheers you or reminds you of someone you love. Your angels will use this type of sign to help you feel better.

Be aware that you can gain excellent guidance through music that comes to you out of the blue. This effect is especially true when you wake up with a song playing in your head and realize that it responds to your request for help from your angels. This kind of nocturnal experience is a clear sign that you had angels visiting you that night.

Behind the Scenes

Angels know everything that is happening behind the scenes, everything that will happen. That does not mean they will share that information with you. It does mean there is a method behind the apparent madness of some of their messages.

My angels knew what "John" was doing without my knowledge. They were aware of the addictive behaviors that were endangering me and the danger to my life. I don't think that way. It would have never occurred to me that someone who purported to love me would hurt me like that. It is entirely due to my angels that I am alive and helping others with their challenges.

Developing Trust

How do you develop trust in your angels? The same way you build trust in your intuition. You pay attention to what your angels say; you follow their guidance and note how that works out for you. Ask yourself these questions:

- Did your angel's guidance help you?
- Did you avoid an unpleasant experience?
- Were you able to shift out of a negative situation?
- Was your life improved?
- Do you feel happier about yourself and/or your life?
- Are you receiving more angelic messages now?
- Is it easier to hear the messages?

It is through noting positive outcomes that you gain more trust in the messages your angels give you. If you only hear them and never act, there is no way to know how the guidance of your angels may have improved your life. You are taking a little leap of faith in following your angels' messages, but the risk of adverse outcomes is higher if you do not act at all.

This issue of trust is why I teach how to hear your angels last. First, I want you to feel them and see them. You need to believe that they are real and with you before you are ready to trust enough to follow what they say.

I did not get there quickly. The difference for me is that I was a toddler when I first recall my angels talking to me, appearing to me, and holding me. I grew up with their undeniable presence. It was, and is, natural to me. Even so, it took me until age 14 to understand that they spoke to me even when I couldn't see them. Then another year or so to start following their guidance better.

Just like any relationship, trust does not happen immediately. It develops over time. Follow one message and note what happens. If you feel happy with the outcome, it will be easier to follow the next. Let this process happen naturally over time so that you can embrace trust wholeheartedly.

You need to come to a place, however long it takes, where you follow the guidance of your angels every time. I don't want to jump ahead, so you will find out why this is important when you get to Chapter 13- Going Rogue. If I can help you avoid going through what I, and others, did, I will consider that mission accomplished.

Exercises

Get Quiet and Ask

Find a quiet place, sit, or lie comfortably and do deep breathing, in through your nose and exhaling through your mouth. When you have achieved a deeply relaxed state, ask your angels a question. It can be about their name, an answer to a question you have, or a message they wish to give you. Remain relaxed for a few minutes to give them time to respond.

If you hear something, do not question it. Sit up and write it in your journal. Make sure to note what you asked your angels as well. This ability is a skill you will gain with frequent practice. A typical message to hear from angels is "eliminate distractions." They know that it is difficult for us to listen to them when there is too much noise or activity around us.

Messages in Music

When you are alone, turn on music with lyrics, not instrumentals. Sit or lie comfortably. Focus on a situation you would like angelic guidance on that is relevant in your life. As you do this, put some awareness on the song lyrics you are hearing. If you note lyrics that speak directly to your situation or mean something specific to you that relates to your dilemma, write it down in your journal.

In Chapter 8, you will learn to recognize the presence of angels by scent and how to use these scents to enhance your connection to your angels.

CHAPTER EIGHT
Scent of Angels

Clairalience

There is a form of extrasensory perception known as Clairalience. This word means "clear smelling." This sense involves receiving spiritual impressions through your sense of smell.

The way you experience it is by smelling a scent that others cannot perceive. There will be no physical explanation for why you smell it, such as suddenly smelling an orange when there are no oranges in the vicinity.

When it Happens

This phenomenon may occur when you are praying, talking to your angels, or meditating. The aroma most reported is that of roses. Smelling this sweet scent is a message to you that you are in the presence of something holy, sacred, and that you are deeply loved.

When you ask your angels for a sign, you are more likely to experience this type of angelic sign. The specific scent you smell can be directly related to the topic you were telling your angels about before noticing the aroma. It is an answer to your request or your question.

Stop and Smell the Roses

You have heard the saying "stop and smell the roses." People say this to others or themselves when they are not taking time to notice the beauty of nature and enjoy the beautiful little moments of life. This phrase goes to a deeper level when you know how often the scent of roses plays a role in angelic encounters.

The scent of roses around you when no roses are near you is a clear sign that an angel is making its presence known to you. It is a sacred scent also associated closely with Mother Mary. She is known as Our Lady of the Roses because the rose is one of her symbols.

When you smell the sweet scent of roses after praying, it is a perceivable reminder of the love your angels have for you. A supernatural experience of smelling roses that are not physically there is a special blessing you are receiving. Do not shrug this off as an odd occurrence. Pay attention to this little miraculous moment.

Difficult to Describe

When you are tuning into the presence of your angels, all your senses are involved. These Divine scents can be wonderful and ultimately indefinable. People who speak for a living cannot come up with words sufficient to describe the smell.

In her book The Color of Angels: Cosmology, Gender, and the Aesthetic Imagination, Constance Classen writes: "... Aside from healing, a variety of wonders are associated with odors of sanctity. Along with their physical powers, odors of sanctity have the reputed ability to induce repentance and offer spiritual consolation. Odors of sanctity could provide the soul with a direct infusion of divine joy and grace.

The divinely sweet scent of the odor of sanctity was deemed to constitute a foretaste of heaven. Angels shared the perfumed nature of heaven. [Saint] Lydwine's hand was left penetrated with fragrance after having held the hand of an angel. [Saint] Benoite experienced angels as birds scenting the air with fragrance."

Other times the scent is immediately known. It may be something you are familiar with or can generally identify the smell.

You may have noticed a subtle scent of something blissful but could not identify what it was or the source. This inability to define the smell can be a sign for you from your angels. They love to make their presence known by emanating a scent.

You will likely be the only one who can smell this scent, even if you are in a room full of people. The smell is a sign for you.

Angelic Scents

Some of the scents associated with angels are:

- An unknown floral fragrance that is also a bit fruity
- Roses
- Lavender
- Lilies
- Herbal

But it's not just a scent that you may notice when an angel wants you to know they are near. Let's talk about how you might feel.

Associated Feelings

There is not one specific angel scent. They tend to use an aroma that means something special to you. It can be unique to you, a smell that gives you a warm, comforting feeling. Maybe that aroma is coffee, cinnamon, vanilla, or freshly baked bread. They know you and will use a scent to give you a sense of comfort and safety before they make their presence known to you.

The scent your angels give to you is always lovely and relaxing. You will feel a sense of their Celestial presence as you become aware of the fragrance. Angels don't always come in with an aroma, you will recognize it for what it is and embrace the gift.

Using Scent to Communicate With Angels

When you want to create a conducive environment for communicating with your angels, you can do this scent. I use Bulgarian rose essential oil for this purpose. I became aware of it's high-frequency property when, in the early 1990s, I visited a Bulgarian monastery built into the side of a cliff wall. The monks there grew the roses and made products with rose oil in them. Just one whiff of this particular type of rose oil lifted me so high spiritually. Angels, in great numbers, came in around me. I knew that discovering this was important for me. I bought all I could afford. Luckily, these products are now available by mail order online.

You can use other rose essential oils that appeal to you. Yes, there are different scents associated with angels, as I listed above. Choose the one which you feel attracted to use. If you are unsure of how to select, do the second exercise listed below.

It's crucial that you use high-quality essential oils and not the cheap synthetic type. Those have a much lower frequency and can produce allergy symptoms.

Here are some methods you can use to enhance your angelic communications:

- Put the scent in a diffuser in the room with you and let it run for at least 10 minutes before you begin.

- Dab a few drops on the lava ball inside an essential oil necklace. Make sure you can easily smell the scent wearing the necklace. You may need a shorter chain.

- Put a few drops on a lightbulb in the room while it's turned off. Please turn it on to warm up the oil and release the scent.

- Spray rose oil water in the air around you before you begin.

Next, I have provided you with some exercises which will assist you in discerning the scents your angels like best.

Exercises

<u>Detecting the Scent of your Angels</u>

Sit quietly in meditation for a few minutes. Consciously release expectations. Then ask your other angels to step back and allow only your Master Guide to remain next to you. Out loud, ask your Master Guide to "Make me aware of your scent, please." Clear your mind and allow any thoughts, pictures, or feelings to enter. Avoid judging anything you receive.

Write it down in your angel journal. You may smell your angel's scent. But you could also be given words or pictures related to it. Your angel may not have a smell. If you try this a few times with no results, ask your angel if they have an essential oil they prefer to use during your time communicating with them.

<u>Learning the Best Scent for You to Use</u>

There are three ways to do this. The first is Muscle Testing. Hold a bottle of essential oil in one hand. Then bend that arm, so your forearm is level with your closed hand facing up. Place your other hand on the forearm of the arm holding the oil. Ask out loud, "Is (insert name of oil) going to help me communicate with my angels more effectively?"

As you push down on your forearm, try to keep that arm steady. If your arm is difficult to impossible to push down, the answer is "yes". The answer is "no" if your arm is easily pushed down. You will likely find this method to be beneficial.

Another method is to use a pendulum. The idea behind this is that there is energy in everything. When using a pendulum, the energy within you runs through your arm and down into the pendulum. The movement corresponds to the frequency of the item or question you are asking.

Using a pendulum can help you gain insight by asking them yes or no questions and seeing how they respond. They help to bring unconscious energy into conscious awareness. Remember that a pendulum can be a long chain necklace with a heavy pendant. Put one bottle of essential oil on a flat surface. Hold the closed clasp between your thumb and forefinger over the bottle. Run your fingers down the chain to still it. Out loud, ask, "Is (insert name of oil) going to help me communicate with my angels more effectively?" Generally, when the pendulum moves in wide circles, you are getting a big "yes," smaller circles mean it will be somewhat effective.

The pendulum standing still means "no."

It's important to know that your "yes" and "no" with a pendulum could be different. If you are new to using a pendulum, first establish this information by saying aloud, "Pendulum, show me my yes." Give it a few minutes to start moving. It does not always happen immediately. Do this a few times to feel confident that you are, indeed, getting your "yes." Repeat this process for your "no." Once you have this down, you can use your pendulum with more confidence. This process is not magic. It's science.

You can also go to a health food store with demo bottles of high-quality natural essential oils. Smell one and see how you feel. Wait a few minutes to clear the first scent before smelling the next one. You could very well have a strong positive reaction to one and be able to take it home and put it to use.

I felt it was imperative to give you specific methods to use if you feel blocked or find you cannot achieve one of the skills taught in this book. It doesn't mean you can't do it. It only means that you have a block inside that has not come down yet.

In the next chapter, you will learn ways to bring that kind of block down, raise your frequency higher and begin to make progress with feeling, seeing, and hearing your angels.

CHAPTER NINE
Troubleshooting

You Can't Force This

One of my terrific clients came back to see me in Sedona a year after her angel reading. She shared with me that she had been "trying so hard" to feel her angels but had not been able to. This woman was frustrated and told me that she thought she could not connect with angels. I calmed her down, and we talked about the things that can get in the way of feeling, seeing, and hearing angels. It turns out she had been trying almost daily for extended periods.

That, combined with getting tense and telling herself that she couldn't do it, had prevented her from making progress. I was so glad she came back to discuss this with me instead of continuing the same way.

When she returned home and began practicing for no more than five minutes and taking a day or so between practice sessions, she began to make progress. It was all about stepping out of stress and letting things unfold naturally.

This lovely lady is not the only person who had this type of experience. Similar reports from clients new to this journey are why I realized I need to include information on preparing yourself and making it easier for you to accomplish these skills.

Breaking Barriers

When you cannot seem to break through your barrier to see, hear or feel your angels, your state of balance is the first place to start. If you are tense, frustrated, or nervous, you will make it more challenging to accomplish the skills you seek to have.

Spend some time doing one of these activities to gain balance and more calm energy before you try any of the exercises again:

- Meditation
- Yoga
- Time in Nature
- Gardening
- Sing or Play a Musical Instrument
- Play Music that Uplifts you
- Dance

Lift Your Spirits

These activities will pull you out of any negative emotions and lift your spirits. A natural result is that your frequency rises, making it easier for you to feel your angels. Start by doing one, or more, of the above activities for an hour or so.

Then, try to feel, hear or see your angels. If you are still feeling stuck, bump things up by doing one of these activities daily. It does not have to be for an hour. I get that life can be busy. Fit in your practice sessions as you can.

Clearing with Essential Oils

If you are still finding it problematic to feel, see or hear your angels, this is the next step to try breaking through your barrier. My favorite clearing method is using essential oils. It is a powerful, sweet-smelling option. Here is how you do this:

I use frankincense, lavender, and rose oil for energy clearing daily for myself and my office and weekly in my home. This method clears the energy and sets the intention that only that of the highest and best good for myself, my family, friends, and workmates, may enter.

Here is a list of some essential oils you can use for energy clearing:

- Rose- Considered the queen of all oils. This sacred substance is the oil with the highest vibrational frequency. The best one is Bulgarian Rose.

- Basil- It has been considered sacred all over most of the world and is well known for its protection when in crowds.

- Cypress- Purifies surrounding energies while uplifting frequency levels at the same time. It will give you a feeling of being grounded and secure.

- Frankincense- Known for purification as well as exorcism. This essential oil removes negative influences in the body, aura, psychic field, and environment.

- Juniper- Ends negativity. It cleanses energies harmful to good health and transform negative energy into positive.

- Lavender- Clears out and neutralizes energies that will not leave your space.

- Myrrh- Purifies the environment. When combined with other oils, it increases their potency.

- Sage- Neutralizes existing negativity and creates a psychic shield against tension. It's used by Native Americans to clear the air of negativity.

- Palo Santo- Legend is that this essential oil carries the sacred Palo Santo trees spirits and is part of what makes the oil so potent. It helps clear buildings of "bad energy" and brings in good luck.

- Peppermint- A powerful astringent used for clearing tension and negative vibes. This refreshing essential oil is an outstanding choice for uplifting a toxic work environment.

- Cedarwood (Virginian)- A majestic tree that expresses a great spiritual strength. This option is what is needed when experiencing a dark energy attack.

You can create a kit for cleansing your energy regularly. Choose three or four which resonate strongly with you. You will be using these one at a time, not mixing them. Keep them in a cool, dry location to ensure they retain their potency.

To do a clearing of your energy, dab a little of each oil on your chakras, saying I release all negative energy and allow only light and love to exist within me and around me. Anything that is not of my best and highest good must leave now. I give myself permission to raise my frequency to the highest level possible for me currently. I say this repeatedly as I put the oil on my chakras.

Then say a little prayer. Here is what I say, though you are welcome to use your own:

"God, surround me in the golden bubble of your love and protection, sealing in my positive energy and sealing out all negative energy and those from the lower realms. I sent white light to the lower realms so only peace and love may remain. Amen."

Open Those Chakras

In Sanskrit, the word chakra means disk or wheel. This term refers to the seven wheels, or desks, of energy centers in your body. A person functions best when the chakras are open and balanced. If they become blocked, a person can experience physical, mental, or emotional issues related to a particular chakra.

The 7 Chakras are:

- Crown- Top of head
- Third eye- Between the eyes
- Throat- Center front of the throat
- Heart- Center of chest
- Solar Plexus- Upper stomach
- Sacral- Just below the belly button
- Root- Base of spine

When your chakras are open and functioning well, you will feel a difference. When your chakras open fully, you can find yourself gaining insight into life-force, feeling compassion for the human race, gaining deeper respect for animals and Earth, or feeling a more intense connection to God/Creator.

You are likely to feel a difference. Each chakra provides a different set of experiences once they are fully open. You will be aware of related levels of the universe and possibly even different worlds beyond the physical.

These are known as parallel worlds or universes or other dimensions.

These sub-planes of the celestial universe are awe-inspiring beyond what we know in the physical world. Through the opening of your chakras, these become available for you to experience.

You may also find that you are gaining insights into the illusive functioning of nature itself. You will likely develop more sensitivity around your five senses, plus the clairs, clear seeing, hearing, feeling, emotion, taste, smell, and touch.

Clairs comes from the French word 'clair,' meaning 'clear.' This refers to an extraordinary ability of one or more of the seven spiritual clairs, such as clear seeing, which exceeds conventional understanding.

A pendulum is a device that responds to the energy of a person, chakra, land, or presence. It can pick up the energy coming from your chakras and give you a visual idea of how open or closed each of your chakras is. It is simply a medium-weight stone at the end of a lightweight chain and a charm at the other end. If you do not have one, you can use a long light chain necklace with a weighted pendant on it.

There are various purposes for a pendulum. The following instructions are specific to determine the state of a chakra and mark your progress. It provides a visible reflection of the state of your chakra.

Next is a method for testing how open each of your chakras are. Hold the pendulum by the charm directly in front of your Crown Chakra and about five inches away, letting the stone end hang down. If you use a necklace, clasp it and hold the clasp in your fingers, letting the pendant hang down below. Run your fingers slowly down the chain to stop any movement. Say, "Show me the current state of my Crown Chakra."

Give some time for the pendulum to show movement. If it goes in a clockwise direction, that is how open your chakra is. If it's wide open, the pendulum will swing in a wide circle which is why you hold it away from yourself. Hold it too close, and you can bonk yourself with it. If the pendulum does not move at all, your chakra is likely blocked.

If your chakra is blocked or not fully open, try one of the following exercises from a post on LearnReligions.com.

Exercises

<u>Visualization</u>

Holding the pendulum still before the chakra, close your eyes and visualize heavy wood doors closed over your chakra. They are tough to open. See yourself pushing from inside, seeing a sliver of light as the doors open a bit. Push harder until those doors are wide open. Then see golden light filling up your chakra, pushing out anything in it that is keeping it from being clear and balanced. Feel your chakra becoming warm and radiating that golden light.

Open your eyes and see what the pendulum is doing. It should begin to swing as your chakra opens. Close your eyes and allow that golden light to continue doing its work. See the doors of your chakra becoming lighter, smoothly opening as needed. Occasionally open your eyes again to see the pendulum movement. Continue until the pendulum swings widely or 10 minutes have passed.

It's not always possible to completely open a chakra in one try. The amount of time involved to open chakras will depend on how much it is blocked, how long it has been blocked, and what led to the blockage in the first place. Severe trauma from long ago takes a while to clear.

<u>Open with Exercise</u>

There are mental and physical exercises specific to each chakra you can use to strengthen and balance your chakras. (1)

- Crown Chakra- Prayer and meditation.
- Third Eye (Brow Chakra)- Lucid dreaming, visualization, and

remote viewing.

- Throat Chakra- Singing, gargling with salt water, or screaming.
- Heart Chakra- Hugging, swimming the breaststroke, or doing push-ups.
- Solar Plexus- Dancing the Twist, hula hooping, or belly dancing.
- Sacral Chakra- Pelvic thrusts and circular pelvis movements; some belly dancing moves provide this movement.
- Root Chakra- Stomping your feet upon the ground, marching in place, or doing squats.
- Aura- Showering, soaking in an Epsom salt bath, smudging with sage/Palo Santo/or essential oils, or deep cleansing breaths.

Meditation

If you practice one, or both, of these exercises more than ten times and experience no pendulum movement, please visit my YouTube channel (Ivory LaNoue) to view the guided meditation on "Opening Your Chakras". You will find the URL in the Celestial Connections of this book.

Meditation is a great way to balance yourself, calm your mind, and become more receptive to angelic presence and messages. Listen to and watch that video daily for a week and try using your pendulum again. Continue this process until your chakras are fully open.

Raise Your Frequency

If another two weeks go by and you still cannot see, hear, or feel your angels, try raising your frequency. This process is about changing your energy or vibration. Everything has a frequency; people, animals, trees, and Earth itself.

The higher your frequency or vibration, the lighter you will feel on every level. Some of the benefits are experiencing greater personal power, clarity, peace, love, and the ability to see, hear and feel your angels.

There are many ways to accomplish this. Here are some of my favorite methods:

Thoughts and Words

You create your reality through your thoughts and words. When a negative idea enters your mind, acknowledge it, ask yourself if you genuinely believe it. If it is beneficial for you, then dismiss it, turn it around by thinking of a positive message.

Meditation and Visualization

Rushing through our days can lead to a state of chaos. Set aside 10-15 minutes daily for meditation or visualization. This practice will help you to find peace, balance, clarity, insight and will reduce anxiety. Visit my YouTube channel for meditation videos that will help you with this. Listen to and watch one of these videos daily for the fastest results. You will find the URL for my YouTube channel in the Celestial Connections section of this book.

High Vibration Books

Find a high-frequency self-help book that speaks to you. Read a chapter every day or so, leaving time to absorb the material and put new concepts into practice. A great book, to begin with, is The Four Agreements by Don Miguel Ruiz.

It's small, easy to read, and contains a lot of great wisdom. Books of this type will leave you feeling better and can transform your life.

Affirmations

Come up with three statements that you want to be true about you or your life. They can be simple, such as "I am happy," or longer such as "I attract loving, healthy people into my life." Twice a day, say them three times, out loud, looking in a mirror. Continue doing this until you realize that you mean what you say. Then you can discard that affirmation and add a new one.

Gratitude

Notice the beauty around you. Twice a day, take a moment to state, out loud, what you are grateful for in life. We all have blessings, and when you focus on them instead of what you don't have your view shifts.

Intentions

Just before you sleep, set an intention about the next day. Imagine feeling happy and having awesome things happening throughout the next day. When you wake in the morning, say, "This is going to be an amazing day. I'm excited and happy." This simple practice will have a powerful effect on your outlook and the outcome of your days.

Be Generous

Cultivate a habit of giving to others without expecting anything in return or seeking credit for it. This practice is not just about money or items. Consider giving of your time. Doing this shifts your thinking from a position of lack to that of having plenty. Abundance is a high vibration position.

Laugh

Frequent laughing improves your mood and quickly raises your frequency. Take a lighthearted approach to challenges in life.

Insert a bit of humor to diffuse situations. If you find yourself having difficulty shaking a negative thought, push it aside and think about an event in the past that made you laugh. Your peace of mind is valuable.

Avoid Violence and Fear

TV, movies, books, and music that involve fear or violence will bring your frequency down. The same is true for conversations on violent topics. Find alternatives that make you laugh, feel joy, tap into kindness, and other high-frequency emotions.

Sending Love

Think of three people who you find challenging. Visualize love going from you to them. Say their name and bless them out loud. This process will probably not be easy to do at first, but it will lift your spirits and your frequency over time. Put these steps into practice. When they have become part of your routine, you are ready for more.

There are many other ways to raise your frequency, such as eliminating toxins from your body in the form of tobacco, alcohol, drugs, pain pills, sugar, excess meat. On the flip side of that, you can gain progress by eating a vegetarian or mostly vegetarian diet, mainly drinking pure water, getting exercise, and spending time in nature.

If you want more information, do an online search for "Ways to increase my frequency or vibration." There are many websites with hundreds of methods. Choose the ones that feel right for you. I suggest you start with just a few, so you don't overload yourself. When those have become a habit, add a few more.

It's Working

When you have been successful in raising your frequency, you will notice one or more of these signs:

- Feeling happier & lighter

- Having an easier time seeing the good in people and the world

- An increase in your spiritual gifts
- Being able to see your angels
- Hearing your angels
- Feeling your angels
- Being less affected by negative energy
- A sense of calm even in a storm

You will likely feel these changes first, followed by others as your frequency continues to rise. I am not suggesting they will happen in the order listed above. Like all other aspects of our journeys, each person will have their own experience in their own time.

Affirmations

Saying affirmations can be a great way to build your confidence and bring down any lingering internal barriers. Here are a few to try:

- I am an open channel for angel communications.
- I hear my angels clearly and easily.
- I give my body permission to feel the touch of my angels.
- Every day, I find that I gain skill in seeing my angels.
- It is easy for me to hear the words of my angels.
- I rise above negative emotions to the highest frequency possible for me at this time.
- I trust the words I hear my angels say are accurate and true.
- I am getting out of my own way and allowing myself to experience my angels fully.

Feel free to write your own. Put your affirmations in your own words, which are comfortable for you to say.

Write three affirmations on a piece of paper and tape it to your bathroom mirror. Every morning and night, say them out loud, looking yourself in the eye, three times each. Say them like you mean them by putting some oomph into your words and fake confidence if need be.

Continue this practice until you realize that you either do mean what you said or overcome that issue. Then replace it with another affirmation until you can feel, see and hear your angels.

If you have gained the ability to feel, see and hear your angels, you are ready for the next step. Again, if not, keep working on the troubleshooting tips until you break through your barriers. It will happen for you. Never give up on having a deep relationship with your angels.

Let's move forward now to learn how to create a close relationship with your angels. Now is when you take the skills you have learned and put them into practice in your life on a day-to-day basis.

CHAPTER TEN
Angels in Your Heart

"Always remember that you are in the presence of your Guardian Angel. In whatever place you may be, in whatever secret recess you may hide, think of your Guardian Angel. Never do in the presence of your Angel what you would not do in my presence." ~St. Bernard, celebrated Abbey of Clairvaux in the 12th century.

Stepping Out of Fear

The client in this story permitted me to relate her experience to you. A client whom I was guiding through the process of stepping into her power and breaking free from a toxic relationship came to see me for the second class in her course. When I last saw her, she was anxious, tearful, and afraid to make a change of any kind.

At this appointment, she was still a little nervous but was smiling. I could feel a positive change in her energy, and I was interested in hearing about her experiences since I last saw her.

She shared with me that she was doing her daily meditation two weeks earlier, and one of her angels had appeared to her. It startled her, but the angel's beautiful appearance and loving frequency kept her in a meditative state. Her angel told her that she needed to let go of her fear. That it was a form of ego, and it was keeping her frozen in place. Her angel let her know that she is not going through this alone. The angel offered to intervene and assist her in creating a new life.

That was a turning point for my client. She felt the powerful presence of her angels around her and understood that she had excellent protection. My client said that she released a huge breath of air and felt a change within herself. She described it as stepping out of fear. She could think clearly, see the steps she needed to take, and felt confident about her ability to do so.

She had a lot of work left to do, but the progress she made from that point was remarkable. It was not that she became a different person. It's more like she remembered who she is and understood that she has an entire team of angels on her side. She exhibited great courage in leaving that relationship and starting a new life for herself. Since then, she communicates with her angels throughout her days, asking them for guidance. She finds herself giving thanks regularly for how they have helped her.

With the guidance of her angels, she reported that her worse fears never came to pass. The divorce was much smoother than she had first thought it would be. This experience left her feeling courage and a sense of calm that she carries with her even now.

Anyone can have this kind of bond with their angels and guides. It does not matter what your ability is now or how far you have gone on your spiritual journey.

As you begin to form a close bond with your angels, you may see symbols of this as you go about your life. Let me tell you about that.

Angel Shapes

When you see something shaped like a meaningful item, it is a little hello from your angels. It can also be a confirmation from them of a thought or idea you were having at that time. They can be hearts, smiley faces, animals, flowers, feathers, or many other possibilities.

Here are some ways you may see these shapes:

- Clouds
- Stones
- Bubbles
- Tea leaves
- Imprints in snow
- Photos
- Pictures
- Paintings
- Blog posts

When you find a specific shape item or see images of it a few times, you receive an angel shape message.

My brother and sister-in-law, Allen and Vicki Jo, find heart-shaped stones everywhere they travel. They have a collection of them. These stones remind them of their love for one another, for family, and those who have passed. It seems they will be walking along; they look down, and voila, there is another heart-shaped stone. Rarely are they looking for these stones in the shape of a heart.

You can find books and websites which offer an interpretation of angel symbols of all kinds. These can be helpful to have on hand as a reference. Because when you are aware you are receiving symbols of any kind, you will begin seeing more of them. Your awareness opens.

When you see an angel image, take a moment to connect what you saw with a recent issue in your life.

Angels Have Longings

Your angels desire a close relationship with you. It is of great sadness that most humans are not aware of their presence, let alone their undertaking to guide and protect throughout our lives.

Your angelic team loves you unconditionally. Your angels are entirely devoted to you; however, they can offer you far more guidance and aid when you exercise your free will. You need to ask. God/Source gave us free will so we can make decisions about our lives. Yes, your angels are watching over you, but they will usually let you continue to exercise free will until you invite them to intervene on your behalf.

This chapter is about bonding with your angels, just as you would bond with a friend. The goal is to strengthen your relationship. Attempting to create this bond lets your angels know that you are aware of their presence and that you are grateful for their love and assistance. Through your efforts, you let them know that you desire more of their love, guidance, healing, and intervention.

Great Expectations

When you invite your angels into your heart and life in a more profound way, they can assist you more often, and in ways that can be dramatic, such as the teenage experience I shared with you.

Taking the time to build this bond results in:

- reduction of fear and stress

- a strong sense of security
- increased confidence
- feeling deeply loved
- gaining a lot of guidance in all aspects of your life
- avoiding negative experiences
- early warning of health issues
- inspiration
- better balance
- peace of mind

If you have been longing for it, now is the time to begin forming a close, personal bond with your angels. Keep reading to learn how to do that, step by step.

Bonding Time

Creating a close relationship with your angels does not need to be a super-serious endeavor. Angels have a sense of humor and, however you choose to bond with them, will be delighted. Feel free to have fun with this. It takes a little time each day and conscious effort to begin this process. Here are some steps to get you started:

Upon waking, greet your angels and thank them for accompanying and protecting you throughout your day. Before you leave for work, errands, or a journey, ask them to provide you with extra protection.

Consider making your request in one of the methods below:

1. "Angels, surround and protect me with your love and light as I make my way today. Let me feel your divine presence and lifted

in the knowledge that I have your divine guidance in all things."

2. Imagine a golden bubble of angelic protection around you, cushioning you from any dangers. Would you mind taking a moment to visualize it and feel the celestial energy around you?

3. I like to request protection as my plane takes off by saying, "Angels guard and protect me as I take this flight today. Make this a calm, uneventful flight. Please help me and everyone on this flight land safely."

4. Throughout your day, occasionally say something like, Angels, I love you and am blessed by your presence. Please help me to feel, see and hear you more clearly every day. Before you pray, take a few moments to feel the presence of your angelic team around you. Ask them to provide you with enlightenment.

5. When you are in bed and ready to sleep, say "Angels surround me, angels protect me." When I say this, I immediately feel the energy of my angels pull in closer to me, providing me with a deep sense of peace and safety.

One of the aspects of the human experience is having free will to make decisions about your life. In the next section, you will find out how to bypass that when you need to.

Free Will

A big part of the human experience is exercising free will. That is, making choices and decisions about your life. Questions such as who you will date or marry, what career you will enter into, friendships you will create, houses bought, vacations, divorces, having children, and any other kind of decision you may encounter.

We learn by exercising our free will and experiencing the results of our choices. This practice is an essential process to gain wisdom, insight and remember to follow our intuition.

It's not healthy or wise to neglect your right to make choices for yourself. No one else can know everything that has happened to you or exactly what you want to achieve. Handing decisions over to someone else is giving away your power and control.

But there are times when you are not able to use your free will. When that happens, you can ask your angels for special assistance or intervention.

Asking for Intervention

You can find yourself deep in trauma, so worn out, sick or confused, that you have no idea what to do. In cases like that, your angels are standing by, ready to help. But they will not interfere, due to your right to exercise free will, unless you ask them to do so.

If you need to do this, say, "Angels, I need you to intervene on my behalf and (insert specific of what you need help with)."

Avoid telling them how to do it or providing too many details. The angels know so many ways to achieve a goal that you cannot even imagine. Why put limits on them in how they help you?

An example of this is a person who has lost their job, is depressed and desperate, and doesn't know how to keep a roof over their family's head.

Their head is spinning with so many fears and what-if's that they can't think straight. They ask their angels for help by saying, "Angels, please intervene on my behalf and bring me the money I need to pay my bills and survive another month."

Within a few days, they receive unexpected money from a family member in exactly the amount needed. This windfall can even be from a person who would not usually send you money.

Your angels will jump into action and begin helping you, understanding that you cannot do it for yourself at this time.

Don't think that you will be bothering your angels. They want you to ask for help when you need it. Your angels long to be of more service to you. They will be singing in their angelic voices with joy at the opportunity of helping you when you need it most.

So far, you have been learning about your angels but do not have names for them. Now, I'm going to help you remedy that with some simple exercises.

Greeting Them

Call your angels by their names. While the angels don't care if you call them by a name or address them as "angels," humans are accustomed to identifying others by name. Addressing your angels by name will help you to create a clear image of your angels. This habit makes them more solid to you, as we humans are accustomed to greeting people by name.

If you don't know their names, it's okay to address them as a group as your angelic team does work together. Sometimes I see an angel pop in and say, "Hello, angels!" They are pleased to be seen and greeted.

If you already know the names of your Master Guide or Guardian Angel, that's great. If not, try one of the exercises below to discover their names. Concentrate on one angel at a time. It's helpful to have paper and writing implement at hand to make a note.

Exercises

Quiet Contemplation Method

Be in a calm place where you can do a few minutes of deep breathing, in through your nose and exhaling thru your mouth in a long, slow breath. Clear your mind. If thoughts pop in, notice them and release them.

Then say out loud, "I invite my Master Guide (or Guardian Angel) to tell me their name." If a name pops into your mind immediately, it was given to you by your angel. Please write it down, so you remember it. If not, try another day again. It is not productive to try to make it happen.

Meditation Method

Be in a quiet place. State your intention of learning the name of your Master Guide or Guardian Angel. Do a few minutes of deep breathing as I described above. Clear your mind. Once you are deep in a meditative state, silently ask to be told and shown the name of your angel. If it is unclear, ask your angel to say it louder and slower, or show you an image again. If you don't get anything or it remains unclear, try another day again.

You will not be able to force this. When meant to receive the name, you will hear or see it. Trying too hard or for too long makes it more difficult to receive information.

Angels can have beautiful names like Celestine, Seraphina, and Lycanciel. But they can also have more familiar names such as Samuel, Sarah, Li, and Lucas. Don't disregard the name you hear just because you have never heard it before. We can get in our own way by hoping for a specific name, overthinking, and doubting the one we receive.

I ask angels to show me their name, as well as telling me. Though I did not request this, their names appear as large metallic gold calligraphy letters on the wall. I have them keep that name there until I can write it down. Sometimes they are long or difficult to spell.

If neither method works for you, refer to the Troubleshooting chapter of this book for ways to break through your unconscious barriers. If, after trying those methods, you have not received the names of your angels, you might want to connect with me for this information. (See Resources)

Now you know the names of your angels or are in the process of learning them. You may be intrigued to know that each angel has its personality.

Angelic Personalities

It takes more time to detect the personalities of each of your angels. It happens through working closely with them and feeling their energy. Just as with humans, each angel has its personality. It comes through in their energy and their words.

When you are communicating with them, you might want to tune in to how their energy feels. Is it soft? Is it powerful? When you hear their messages in your head, are they gentle? Perhaps they are insistent, or they inject humor.

You may learn that your Master Guide has an austere nature and communicates with you in direct, concise messages. Your Guardian Angel may have a softer personality and speak more lovingly.

When you communicate with your Joy Guide, they will likely be high energy, playful and fun. A Protector Guide can prove to be stern, speak little, and have intense energy. Make a note of your discoveries in your angel journal (Chapter 4). Eventually, you will know this information as well as the personalities of your family and friends.

You have likely heard of creating sacred space. When you want to grow closer to your angels, it is helpful to create something meaningful to keep that goal at the forefront of your awareness.

Creating Angelic Space

Place an angel statue or painting in your home. Put your angel item in a place you will see it often. It's fun to search for just the right piece that calls out to you, "I'm the one." My office is filled with angel art which makes me feel so happy. At home, I have a lovely angel statue holding a tray. I have placed crystals in that tray specific to angels such as Celestine, Angelite, Clear Quartz, Rose Quartz, Amethyst, Aquamarine on top of a bed of blue glass beads. Around the base of the statue, I scattered more of the blue glass baubles.

Every time you look at your unique angel art piece, you will remember the loving presence of your angelic team. It is a gentle reminder to speak with your angels, thank them, and feel gratitude.

I have noticed that angels appear more frequently near my angel statue than in other places in my home. My work office is so full of angel art that angels pop in everywhere.

Now you will learn the different ways that angels communicate with you. This information will help to ensure you get the total value of their guidance.

CHAPTER ELEVEN
Guidance From Your Angels

Warning!

In the 90's, I was supervising step-down units for psychiatry patients. A couple of my staff members left for other positions, leaving me in having to fill in for some shifts as well as overseeing the facilities. In that exhausting time, I hired two men who were well educated and said all the right things in their interviews. Unfortunately, due to a chronic lack of sleep, I was unable to hear my angels as clearly as I usually would.

A couple of weeks into their employment, I noted their clear disrespect toward me and had a discussion with them about it. I spoke of this with my supervisor, knowing she could do nothing at that point. But I wanted her to be aware of the situation.

Shortly after that, I saw that they were overly attentive to a young female patient in one of the acute units. At first, they were only talking with her frequently. Later, I began to pick up an undercurrent that put me on alert. It was not clear yet, but my angels kept drawing my attention to these two men. I was uncomfortable with their behavior and kept a close watch over them and the patient.

The young female was discharged from the unit soon after that. I heard there two men talking about seeing her at her home after work. I confronted them on this, and they denied saying it. From that moment, both my intuition and my angels were on high alert. Again, I spoke with the director about the situation, and because I had no proof, she said there was nothing she could do.

I instructed the two male staff members to have no further contact with the female patient. They agreed though I was aware they were resentful and almost hostile. A few days later, I heard this same young female patient was in our in-patient unit. She was going to be sent to one of my step-down units the next day. I went to see her in preparation for this change and saw the two problem male staff members existing her room.

My reaction was astonishment and anger. I told these men to leave and that I would speak with them back at the step-down unit shortly. Instead, they argued with me and made it clear that they would not follow the clinic's rules. The director was also concerned about their actions but said she could not take disciplinary action because there was no proof they had done anything beyond disregarding my instructions by seeing her on the in-patient unit.

My angels were on top of this. They were telling me these two men were sexually abusing the female patient. She was afraid to talk about it, and the men denied everything. I did not see this with my eyes, but my intuition and angels were certain that it was true.

Those same two men filed a complaint against me with Human Resources, saying that I had issues with men. I was reprimanded for not treating them equally though my other male staff strongly refuted their charges against me. The two abusers had taken this action solely to stop an investigation from happening which would expose their actions.

My angels told me that the men in the upper administration of this clinic were not going to listen to me or the female director. They valued the word of men above that of women. My angels told me to leave that position or I would suffer a severe physical ailment. Several other managers had died or gone on disability due to stress on the job in the prior year. I knew the pressure was tremendous, but after my angels told me this, I could see that my time there needed to end.

If my angels had not intervened, I would have stuck it out, continuing to push for an investigation and getting nowhere. That was a touch fact for me to face. Then, a few months later, it came out in the news that two men at that facility had been molesting a female patient. Yes, it was my former problem male staffers and the same young female patient. It turned my stomach to read this news. I felt anger at both my helplessness in the situation and the lack of response from upper management. But I felt her angels had interceded to protect her.

At that point, I knew the police and legal system were dealing with the abusers. I was able to let go of worry about that and put my attention toward helping the patient. Daily I prayed for the young woman and asked her angels to help her heal from her trauma.

Quickly I got a position with a foundation that instantly relieved me from the pressures I experienced the previous year. I poured myself into my work with dual-diagnosis patients, meaning they have a mental illness and a learning disability. I was able to begin healing.

The assistance and wisdom from your angels can help you in many ways. Here are some of them:

- It can wake you up to a situation
- Help you realize you need a change
- Point out a toxic person in your life
- Bring your attention to a new career
- Direct you to your life purpose

- Help you recognize an incredible new love

The tricky thing is that you may miss some angelic assistance unless you spend time in quiet meditation or contemplation regularly, or ask for messages or signs. So, let's talk about that a bit.

Easily Overlooked

Because you hear your angels as thoughts in your head, it can be challenging to sort out whether it's your thought or an angel talking to you. This dilemma is especially true when you are first listening to their words.

Remember to pay attention when you are surprised by a thought you have. If it seems odd, not something you would ordinarily think of, or entirely out of context from your thinking, it is likely an angel speaking to you.

You may be expecting their words to be flowing and loving and holy. Sometimes they are. But generally, they are down-to-earth and straightforward. You may hear "Don't go," "Call your mom," or "You need to reread Ivory's book." I'm kidding about that last one. But angel's messages are designed to get your attention fast.

Messages can seem goofy or even funny. Angels have a sense of humor. I've heard plenty of funny messages from my angels, like "That woman's a pickle." Sometimes I listen to them laughing at something I did, said, or experienced. That always gets me laughing with them.

When you think you hear an angelic message, say, "I hear you, angels. I will follow your guidance." I mentioned it before, but the angels don't care if you address them by name. They work as a unit a lot. It's perfectly fine to address them as "angels." I asked my angels if they minded that, and they just laughed.

The more messages you catch and thank your angels for, the more messages you will be given. Yes, angels do talk, but they use a variety of methods to seek your attention. We're going to dive into those ways now.

Angelic Communications

Angels use a variety of methods to get messages to you. If you hear their spoken words, you will get a lot of them. If they are eluding you, you will receive more signs to try and get your attention.

The primary methods are:

- Spoken word
- Written word
- Repetitive Numbers
- Manifesting
- Dreams
- Sensations

You will better understand what to look for because I will discuss these methods in this chapter. Being aware of your angels' different ways to get your attention and pass messages on to you makes you a much more receptive vessel.

Your angels know you so well. They understand how your mind works, what you tend to notice, and what your talents are. Knowing these things, they find ways to work with that, giving you a better chance of getting their guidance.

Let's start with a common form of angelic communication, which is them speaking to you.

Spoken Word

If you like to read, are a writer in any form, or enjoy conversation, you are likely to receive guidance in this form. That does not mean you will not receive signs in different ways.

Some examples of spoken word guidance are:

- Hearing the same message or phrase, repeated in conversations you have with people over a short period.

- Overhearing others talking about a message or thought you have had recently.

- Hearing a song on the radio, on a CD, or at a concert that includes lyrics reinforcing a message you've been getting or a thought you have had recently.

- Hearing song lyrics that directly address emotional distress or a traumatic situation you are going through.

- Seeing or hearing newscasts, movies, and tv shows where a message or recent thought you have been having is talked about somehow.

Your angels continue talking to you directly. But if you are not catching those messages because you are distracted by playing music, they are likely to take advantage of that music by ensuring the directive comes to you that way. You are focused on the music, so you have a better chance of catching the message.

You need quiet time to have a better chance of receiving your angel's spoken messages. Your angels will make their messages more blatant if you are doing anything distracting.

An easy solution is to set aside time for daily meditation. When your mind is clear from distractions, your angels' messages are easier to hear and more apparent to you. When you are ready for a deep relationship with your angels, you owe it to them and yourself to have daily, distraction-free time with them.

I have created a daily meditation for you and posted it on my YouTube channel. You will find that URL in the Celestial Connections section of this book. Watch and listen to it daily, preferably in the morning. This guided meditation will significantly assist you in opening up to messages from your angels. You will be aware that you are receiving them and likely feel surprised at how often you do.

They understand that our world is overstimulating and offers many distractions, but that is a big part of how we have lost a big part of our connection to angels. It was a long, slow slide over hundreds of years. It takes time to form better habits that encourage open communication between you and your angels.

When you receive a message, eliminate any distractions you can. Turn off the television or music, go to a quiet place. Let your angels know you are ready to receive their message. Write it down in your Angel Journal.

While you seek messages and information from your angels, you need to know that you will not always be thrilled to get it.

Not Always Welcome

As I mentioned earlier in this book, angelic messages can be annoying. My angels know the specific instances I am about to share with you. It's funny now, but at the time, I got a bit testy about it.

The first one is one I mentioned earlier in this book. I was trying to get through each day, overwhelmed with stress, fear, and illness. My angels were saying, "You need to write a book. You need to host a talk show." At first, I was intrigued. After months of this, I was flat-out irked.

This chaotic time reminded me that angels have never been human.

They have no concept of stress or illness. It occurred to me that I needed to be clear about my situation. So, I said, "Angels, I hear you and honor your guidance. I will act on it, but I cannot do it now. As soon as I possibly can, I will move forward as you want me to."

The messages continued but slowly became less frequent. By the way, this is the book they told me to write. I hosted the talk show for years and am now hosting another podcast called The Angel Room. My angels are so happy.

Another instance is when I was standing in line at a grocery store in my town. The line was quite long. I noticed an older man, two people behind me. My angels said, Talk to that man. I hear them clearly but did not want to talk to this stranger. I am shy until I get to know a person.

My angels did not care about that. Talk to him. He needs your help. Oh, my goodness! It went on for 10 minutes, constantly until I begged pardon of the lady behind me in line and asked the gentleman if I could have a word with him when he was through the line. He looked surprised and confused but said yes.

We stepped outside the store and found a quieter place to talk. I explained that my angels directed me to speak with him. He was receptive to this. It turns out that his beloved wife had passed away the proceeding week. He was devastated and thinking that he did not want to live anymore. His angels then passed messages to me from his wife. He clasped my arm, looked into my eyes, and began to cry. He thanked me over and over, and I felt his grief lift immensely. We parted, and as I drove by him in the parking lot, he waved and gave me a big smile.

My angels knew that man needed intervention that I could provide. They were not going to stop telling me to talk to the man until I did it. If this kind of thing happens to you, understand that there is an urgent need. Surrender to the will of your angels and do what they guide you to do as soon as you can.

Let's move on to signs, as this is another common form of communication from your angels. You will want to be on the lookout for these. We will start with the times when you are most likely to receive angelic signs.

Transformation Time

You can receive signs from your angels any time, but they tend to be more frequent when you are in specific situations. Your angels are attracted to your rising vibrations, and so these signs happen.

Here are some of the life challenges that can bring on more angelic signs:

- A spiritual awakening
- Coming to a deeper understanding of yourself
- Expansive thinking of the Universe
- Opening up to deep caring for all humanity

It's also likely that you will receive more signs when you are experiencing certain emotions. This intervention is due to your angels' desire to help you shift out of what you are going through. They want to help you.

These are some emotions that can elicit an increase in angelic signs:

- Feeling lonely or isolated
- Sad
- Confusion
- Abandoned
- Vulnerability

Your angels will tune into that and understand that you need extra support. They will help you to know that you play a part in a grand master plan. Everything is happening for a reason, including the circumstances that led to your current emotions.

Feelings are fleeting. They come and go, but sometimes you get stuck. Angels can pry you out of an emotional rut to free you to grow and thrive.

Just reconnecting with the pure love which you carry in your soul can help you rise above a lot of turmoil. When it happens, accept it as a gift of immense love.

Signs can happen when you don't expect them but when you need them most. Sometimes you are not aware of how much you require the assistance.

You are most likely to see signs from your angels when you are in a period of transformation, in the process of becoming your authentic self, or in need of additional love and care.

Signs

When you are on a spiritual journey, you can receive signs to help you along the way. Some situations that can lead to those signs are:

- Working toward the discovery of your mission or life purpose.
- Realizing you have wandered off your path and being ready to align with it again.
- You are moving in the wrong direction.
- Knowing you are ready to heal from trauma.
- You need to experience unconditional love.

Your angels want to reinforce your belief in yourself. Their desire to see you move in the direction will bring you the most joy, fulfillment, and abundance in all aspects of your life.

Angels use a lot of signs and symbols to communicate with you. Sometimes these get through when words do not. They do try talking to you first. Your angels will repeat messages. But if you are not hearing them, understanding they are coming from your angels or ignoring them, your angels will move on to signs.

Know that when you receive a sign from your angels, there is usually something meaningful behind it. A signal may arrive as a flash of inspiration, hearing a message out loud, or experiencing a sudden breakthrough. Your angels send signs to reinforce your thoughts and experiences, give support, and let you know that positive changes and blessings are coming your way.

You now have some idea of the times when you can expect an angel to appear. You are also aware that when you need your angels, you can encourage them to appear.

Know that there more specific circumstances that elicit responses from angels. Keeping these in mind will help to make you more aware of any helpful angel symbols that may be about to appear. If you keep these in mind it will help to make you more aware of the helpful angel symbols that may appear.

We will begin with the most common type of sign which is words.

<u>Words</u>

Angels will use words to give you messages and to confirm your thoughts and ideas. They are creative in how they do this. It goes beyond the spoken word.

Here are some ways you may receive this type of sign:

- Reading a word or phrase that echoes a recent thought.

- Seeing a word on a license plate, billboard, menu, bus, magazine cover, or another place that means something to you or repeats a thought or idea you had.

- Overhearing conversations that are about something you have been mulling over.

- Hearing the same song over and over. Listen to the lyrics carefully for messages meant for you.

- Finding a song coming to your mind or lips frequently. Again, think about the lyrics, as there is likely a message there for you.

Years ago, I was feeling emotionally exhausted. I was in the shower, letting the water run over my head to try and wash the emotions away. My tears ran down with the water. Suddenly, I found myself singing, "I'm the man who loves you, inside and out." It wasn't like I had been thinking of that song or was even in the mood for singing. But the song burst out of me. I felt the energy of my Master Guide surrounding me and knew he had sent those lyrics to me to remind me that I was not alone. I kept singing and felt better.

I began to laugh with joy and felt myself take a step out of despair. It was beautiful to be able to laugh again. I felt a ray of light at that moment. It turns out that it was a turning point for me in my healing. My Master Guide was there at the lowest point for me, letting me know how much he loves me. That kind of support is there for you too.

Let's talk about how the angels use symbols in communicating messages to you.

Symbols

Angels may give symbols in images of angels with wings, halos, and flowing robes. Your angels do this to remind you that they are with you, that they exist, and they have a deep unconditional love for you.

Angels are aware that humans associate divine beings with this type of image. Though it is not how they look in the Celestial Realm, they can use it to get your attention. When you start seeing angel images more frequently than usual or in unexpected places, it's a heads up for you. They are trying to get your attention.

Seeing angel images is often their way of reminding you that you have a powerful team of angels watching over you. They want to remind you that you have incredible support available when you ask for it.

Angel imagery can include images of items associated with angels, such as:

- Halo
- Trumpet
- Angel wings
- Dove
- Sword
- Chalice

You may see a photo of something related to angels, something shaped like one of them, or figurines. When you see them more often than usual, pay attention as you receive symbols from your angels.

Let's move on to a type of sign that emanates from within.

<u>Inner Push</u>

Sometimes angelic signs come from within you. You may feel a strong urge to take a class, visit a city, talk to a person, call a specific person, drive a different route, skip a planned event, renew a hobby, switch careers, join a social group or study a topic.

These are not random whims. When this happens, consider it a sign and follow it. Most of the time, you will not see why it's necessary or where it will lead. Trust that your angels know and that it is in your best and highest good to follow that urge.

It's easy to push these aside and go on with your life. That choice is up to you. Understand that you can receive some of the most important messages this way. Respect your urges.

An example of this is this book. Running a business keeps me very busy. Add to that, seeing my incredible clients and mentoring students. But I kept feeling an urge to write this book. Yes, I was hearing my angels pushing me to write. But I also felt an inner urgency to write every chance I could. I knew my angels said it was essential to get this book published now. I felt it deep inside, and the drive to write was with me always.

You may also see signs from your angels in a visual form.

<u>Angel Shapes</u>

I wrote about this extensively in Chapter 10. Refer to that chapter for details. It's about seeing items shaped like angels, wings, or other angelic symbols.

Another powerful type of angel sign comes in the form of numbers.

<u>Angel Numbers</u>

You may see the same series of numbers repeatedly. When it happens three, or more times, you are seeing Angel Numbers. There are many ways these signs show up. Here are a few:

- Repeatedly your attention is drawn to a clock at a specific time.
- Finding yourself waking up at 2:22 night after night.
- Seeing the same numbers (111, 3333, 444) on license plates,

billboards, tv ads, and online.

- Being given the same numbers for hotel rooms, reservation numbers, etc.

Single and double-digit numbers seen frequently can be signs. Here are common meanings for some of them. Because you are unique with your own experiences, what it means for you could be a bit different. Follow your intuition.

0 (zero)- Angels are giving you divine reassurance.

1- Keep your focus on the positive aspects of your life.

2- You are on the right path, exactly where you are meant to be at this time.

3- Your angels are trying to get your attention.

4- Angelic Healing is available to you.

5- This is an ideal time for a change in your life.

6- Reduce your focus on material items and making money.

7- Right now, you are fortunate. It's a lucky time to take a calculated risk.

8- You are attracting abundance and prosperity.

9- This is an excellent time to act on your dreams.

10- Step forward into new beginnings with optimism.

11- Your intuition will help you make the right decision.

12- Look to new experiences with optimism.

13- You are shifting forward faster on your spiritual journey.

The numbers you see again and again have significant meaning for you. You may be excited to see the same numbers repeatedly, but you are not getting the entire message until you learn the deeper meaning behind them.

The more the numbers repeat, the more critical the message for you is. Remember that angels use numbers to get your attention when you cannot hear them speaking to you, or you are not attributing the message to your angels.

If your angels feel you must receive a message, they will bump up the number of times you see it in a more vigorous attempt to get your notice.

I have a go-to site for angel numbers. You will find that site in the Celestial Connections section at the end of this book. On this site, by Joanne Wharmley, you will find interpretations for numbers zero to 10,000.

When I visit Joanne's website, I feel the high frequency of her messages. Angels come in the verify the accuracy of her words. Joanne's website is the angel number site I refer my clients and students to. Joanne has created a fantastic resource for you to use when you believe you are receiving angel numbers from your angels.

Many signs from your angels come as something you feel on your body.

<u>Sensations</u>

There are several signs that you could feel. I'll explain each of them, so you have a better chance of recognizing them as signs from your angels. The first is an unmistakable sign. It is getting chills out of nowhere.

Sudden Chills

You can be sitting quietly, reading a book. Suddenly your entire body is covered in goosebumps. Chances are you have experienced this and did not consider it may be your angels trying to get your attention. But this is a frequent sign that your angels are attempting to communicate with you.

This sign is a prompt for you to give attention to what you are currently doing, seeing, talking about, or thinking of when you get chills like this. It's not always a warning.

This sign can also be your angels' way of letting you know that you are on the right path or having a fantastic idea. For example, if you are interviewing for various career openings and you get chills when you sit down for one of them, it can mean that you have found the right opportunity. This type of sign is often associated with looking at places to live, thinking of places to move to, mulling over people to date, or deciding where to put the bulk of your time and energy.

I have noticed that if my angels feel it's an excellent opportunity for me, they will give me such intense chills they hurt. I experience these chills if my angels are concerned about me, as well.

Next up is the ringing of the ears.

Ringing Ears

This ringing demands my attention because it comes in so loudly in my left ear. It is a sign I receive frequently. The following section will teach how your perception can be changed while receiving an angelic sign.

Refer back to Chapter 7 where I covered this sensation in detail.

Next, I'll tell you about a sensation that you probably have felt and did not realize was from your angels.

Gentle Breeze

You may be sitting in a room with no fans on, no windows or doors open. The air conditioning or heating is not running, and yet you feel a gentle breeze move around or past you. There is no explanation for this air movement. That is a heads-up that you have angels moving around you, trying to get your attention.

Your angels are creating this breeze. I have this happen every night when I'm doing my intentions before bed. When I sit down to begin, there is no air movement of any kind. I start, and immediately, I feel the breeze stirring around my legs. It grows stronger when I talk about important issues in my life.

It helps a lot to be quiet and relaxed when you are looking for this sign. You are most likely to feel this gentle breeze:

- When you are praying
- Talking to your angels
- Doing intentions
- Working on forgiveness
- Meditating

Pay attention to your emotions and make a note of them in your journal so you can note any patterns.

After I turn off the light at night, I talk with my angels for a while. First, I see them, then I feel their frequency, and then the breeze begins. It is a tangible sensation of movement you can't miss if you are looking for it.

Sometimes it happens when you are thinking about something that's been bothering you. For me, I feel this breeze almost nightly as I get ready for bed. My nightly ablutions have become a bit lengthy. So, I have plenty of time to think about my day, projects, conflicts I've experienced, worries, and people I miss.

My angels come swooping around me. I know they want me to let go of all of that so I can sleep better. The chances are that you have been experiencing this angel breeze and did not know what it was. Now that you do, you will begin connecting that to your angels and the furthering of your connection with them.

Crown Chakra Tingles

A clear angel sign is a tingling sensation on your Crown Chakra, which is the top of your head. You may also feel a sense of warmth in the area. This sensation is a beautiful sign to receive because it reminds you of the high frequency of your angels.

Angels exist in a realm that is far above the physical. When you feel the tingles or warmth in your Crown Chakra, it means your angels are assisting you in opening that chakra so you can receive their high-frequency transmission, wisdom, and downloads.

This type of sign does more than facilitating a wide-open Crown Chakra. Your angels may also adjust your chakra to open up your ability to link with the higher realms. This chakra opening will allow you to communicate with them much better.

There was a time when I felt that tingling every day, off and on through the days. I had no idea what it was. It did not occur to me to ask my angels. I thought it was some kind of nerve damage. Mostly I ignored it. But later, I went back to my journal and realized that it began a year before I had another significant shift forward on my spiritual journey and with my spiritual gifts.

It still happens now and then. Now I know that I am simply receiving information that will come into play in my life when the time is right. I relax and let it happen.

Your Crown Chakra plays a vital role in perceiving the angelic realm. It makes sense that your angels would want to help you unblock that chakra and make it as receptive as possible.

Now that you know what that tingling and warmth sensation is, a sacred gift, you can embrace it.

The next sign from angels affects your entire perception of life and the world.

<u>Enhanced Perception</u>

One of the most impressive changes you can experience when receiving a sign from your angels is enhanced perception and sharpened intuition.

You may experience one or more of these results when you feel angels around you or receive a sure sign:

- Feeling more alive and vibrant
- Seeing colors as more vivid
- Nature looks more beautiful
- Feeling the emotions of others
- Strong intuitive thoughts
- A sense of being slightly high, with no chemicals involved

Underlying abilities are often suppressed. The mere presence of angels can help to strengthen those gifts. Having these reactions to angelic signs can connect you with your spiritual side quickly and powerfully.

Now you will find out how you can receive signs as you sleep.

<u>Dreams</u>

Your subconscious mind more easily receives messages while you sleep because your conscious mind is resting. Because of this, angels often find it easier to communicate with you at this time.

Be alert for recurring dreams, repeating themes and images, and feeling like your dream was important. It may feel like more than just a dream. This feeling is particularly true when you have a precognitive dream.

That is when you dream about something happening, and then, later, it happens just as you saw it in your dream.

For instance, six years ago, I had a dream that most of the state of California was on fire. It was burning out of control. In my dream, I was terrified but determined to fight the fire with every bit of energy I had. Years later, in 2020, there were so many fires in California that it immediately brought my dream back into my mind. I looked back in my dream journal to remind myself what I had seen in my nightmare.

Luckily, I did not have to fight the fires with endless buckets of water, as I was doing in my dream.

That was not the first precognitive dream I had that involved nature. But you may have dreams that are about you, your family, friends, work, travel, your town, the country, or the world.

For me, precognitive dreams are more vivid than my usual vivid dreams. They are so real. I can feel the wind, smell smoke, touch things, and feel the texture. When I wake, I know I need to pay attention to what I experienced. I make a note of these dreams and suggest you do the same. Again, it's helpful to see when you had the vision and exactly what you saw or experienced.

This type of dream is also known as a prophetic dream. There are many examples of historical figures who had such dreams that later came true.

One of the most famous is Abraham Lincoln, who dreamed of his death just days before being shot and killed.

You receive these powerful signs from your angels for a reason. Honor them. Sometimes to warn you, and other times to let you know what is coming to give you time to make plans.

The next type of sign is a physical item, feathers.

<u>Feathers</u>

Finding white feathers have long been associated with the presence of angels. No matter where you find one, know that they are a reminder of your angels' presence, love, and support.

When you find them in strange places, take note. This occurrence means that your angels are trying to break through to your conscious mind and get your attention fast.

Some of the odd places I have found white feathers are:

- In the butter dish in my refrigerator
- Inside of a long-closed jewelry container
- On a counter that was feather-free moments before
- In a shoe
- On top of my jewelry box, where no feather was present earlier
- A trail of them on a sidewalk, leading to a beautiful angel statue

But no matter where you find white feathers, collect them. I find it very comforting to pull out my collection and touch them when I need extra angel love.

Feathers given as a sign may not always be physical feathers. You can find feathers printed on clothing, posters, cards you receive, on the side of a building, a logo, on a product you purchase, and many other places. So, keep your eyes open for these beautiful reminders of how very much your angels love and care about you.

While writing this book, my outstanding writing coach, Parthenia Hicks of KN Literary, related this beautiful story to me that she experienced. She was having a hard time making a particular decision. It was her habit to go on solo walks to think. Over time she realized that every time she was on a walk and sat down to think, she would find a feather, or a group of them, by her foot.

Often it would be the only feather in sight. Whatever decision Parthenia was thinking about at the time, seeing the feather would be her sign of "that's the one." She has had this happen so many times, she now trusts it.

The following sub-section is about the scent of angels.

<u>Divine Scents</u>

This section is about smelling a scent associated with angels. There is a variety of them. You may notice one of the scents with no explanation, and you can use these scents to encourage angelic interaction.

Refer to Chapter 8, where I covered this type of sign in detail.

Earlier in this book, I mentioned angel people to you. It's time for you to learn more about these people, what they can do to help themselves and others.

CHAPTER TWELVE
Angel People

Divine Realm Connection

I remember the first time my client, Ashley, came to see me. Her connection to angels was evident to me, and she confirmed that she had been aware of it for as long as she could remember.

Ashley radiated light. Her frequency is very high, and it was clear to me right away. When I called in the Archangels for spiritual protection, they came in gangbusters. The power of their energy took my breath away. I had intense chills from head to toe.

I asked her Master Guide to stand to her left side, and immediately she was surrounded by a massive light of her angel's energy. It was uncomfortable to look at because it was so bright. This bright light happened with every angel I communicated with on her behalf.

Everything was magnified during her angel reading. She is undoubtedly an angel person. Ashley understood that she has a connection to the Celestial Realm. The Celestial Realm is the place where angels reside. She told me of her experiences and wondered if she was supposed to do something with her gift.

Her ability is unique in that her angels send her spirit to people who need her help. She sees and hears them, and they see and hear her. She is not always sure of where she is at the time, just that her angels have sent her to help. Ashley calms these people and gives them support in their situation. Afterward, she is transported back to where she was before.

Ashley exists. She is not just an example. Hello Ashley! Yes, I have her permission to talk about her a bit. She is a client and student of mine who, like me, has had a strong relationship with angels since early childhood. Ashley is working toward having her own fascinating angel practice.

Humans, Not Angels

Just as some people are born with perfect pitch, the ability to run faster than most, or remember everything they have ever read, some are born with the ability to see, hear and feel angels. It's just another gift from God. It does not make a person better than anyone else, but it does allow them to achieve the full benefit of the presence of their angels early in life.

An angel person is not an angel. They never were an angel. But they have a spiritual gift from God that gives them natural access to angels and guides.

Recognizing This Gift

At the beginning of this chapter, I shared Ashley'[s story with you. But there are other signs of being angel people.

At times I am given a visual sign of a person's close connection to angels. For example, I recall a specific female client who I was seeing for the first time. She was having a Meet Your Angelic Guides session with me.

As I tuned in to her, I told her that she has a special bond with angels.

She confirmed this, and I saw an undulating shower of twinkling stars coming from the ceiling over her head. That was a new experience.

This client was aware that she had a connection to angels but had not explored it or developed it beyond her natural ability. Our session seemed to be a kind of awakening for her as she left, intending to put a lot more energy into discovering what she could do with this gift.

Recently I had an initial session with a beautiful lady who was part of a group of friends. My first glance at her told me that she was a Lightworker. Quickly in her reading, the Archangels came in with more significant energy than usual, and the room remained full of divine energy throughout her session. She was not aware of her special connection to angels but was delighted to hear it. She has been seeking a bigger purpose in her life and is ready to make a change.

Her angels had a lot to say to her. They encouraged her strong desire to help others and give her life more meaning through her work. She lit up with a big smile when she heard that they are already guiding her to her mission. At that moment, her frequency raised even higher.

Another thing Angel People share is a history of surviving situations that could have easily led to their death. Seven incidents and accidents could have easily killed me. But here I am, alive and well.

Other Angel People have reported similar "charmed lives" where they survived perilous experiences or severe injuries. When you are born into your life solely to complete a spiritual mission, you will live to complete it.

Use it for Yourself

If you recognize yourself in any of the examples given above, that does not mean you are obligated to do angel work for a living. What you do with your gift is up to you. Many choose to use it in their personal life.

First, you will find it easier than most to feel, see and hear your angels. You were born with this gift. For you, it's more about enhancing that natural gift as much as you desire.

Here are some of the ways those angel people tell me they use their gift:

- Guidance for themselves
- Insight about family members and friends
- Words to use in attempts to diffuse situations
- Confirmation of their intuition
- A deepening of their relationship to God/Source
- Increased trust
- Building their inner core of strength
- Protecting themselves from negativity
- Remaining calm in the face of difficulty

Some feel a strong inner push to share their gift with others. An angel person can intentionally develop their natural talent of a connection to angels. It's no different than a born psychic choosing to increase their skills to a higher level.

You can take your gift to the highest level possible. Your angels will tell you if that is part of your path and will let you know when you have gone as far as you can. Again, they know everything behind the scenes, so trust them when they tell you it's time to stop training and begin doing your work.

What will that work be? Here are some options, though it's certainly not a complete list:

- Give angel card readings
- Become an angel communicator
- Incorporate angelic messages into other readings
- Add divine communications to your healing, medical or counseling work
- Create a blog about angels
- Host a podcast about angels
- Write a book about angels from your unique perspective

No one path suits every person. Each of us has our direction to take. You may begin using your gift one way, and your angels will lead you to use it differently over time.

Your current comfort level with your ability and your readiness to share it with others will dictate what you are guided to do. If you are confident and eager to share your gift, you will likely propel forward as you wish. But if you are nervous and worry that you can't do it, your journey will take more time.

If that latter description fits you, instead of pushing yourself into doing the work, put your energy into building your confidence. There are specific ways to do this. You will find a couple of exercises in the next chapter.

What if it takes you years to get there? It's not a race. This process is about growing, expanding, and stepping assuredly into your role. My experience with students is that you will go forward, full steam ahead when you are ready.

That fear will go away when you get better at your skills. Nothing beats practice to gain confidence. Because getting positive feedback from people on your work, you become sure about your ability. It comes to a point where you are so confident in the information and messages you get from angels that even if the client in front of you is saying, "No, that's not true.", you know in your heart that it is, and when this person is ready to face it, they will embrace what their angels had to say.

You won't take it personally but move on to the next client with intentions to work from a place of holiness and reverence. You will know that you are doing good and pleasing your angels with your mission. Most of all, you will satisfy yourself. Remember, you came into this life with a mission. Finding it and doing the work is everything.

In the following chapter, you learn the dangers of ignoring the advice of angels.

CHAPTER THIRTEEN
Going Rogue

His Mother Warned Me

In my freshman year of college, I was eighteen years old when I began dating a handsome guy we'll call "Daniel" who, like me, was involved in local theatre productions. He took me to his family's business to meet his parents. They were warm and welcoming, and I felt comfortable with them right away.

Toward the end of a year of dating, "Daniel" asked me to marry him. I accepted. On the next visit with his family, his mother took me aside and said in a low tone, "Don't marry my son." I must have looked as startled as I felt because she then said, "There is something missing in him. He does not know how to feel." At that, I was silent. My brain told me that she did not like me, did not think I was good enough for her son. She continued, "He is not the one for you. If you marry him, it will be the worst mistake of your life." I wanted to cry but waited until I was home to break down. Never did it occur to me that she was trying to help me.

Though I was young and naïve, I had seen red flags within "Daniel's" behavior through the time we were dating. I chose to ignore them. My angels were telling me to walk away. They said that "Daniel" was not who I thought he was. I decided to ignore them too.

The evening before our wedding, my good friend Frank called. He said, "Don't marry him. You don't really know him. This marriage is a mistake." I trusted Frank but knew him to be dramatic. In my mind, it was too late to cancel the wedding. My angels told me to listen to Frank. Again, I chose to ignore them.

It was not long after the marriage when I knew I had made a terrible mistake. "Daniel" was extremely controlling and had begun being violent, throwing heavy items around our tiny apartment. My new husband would verbally and emotionally abuse me, saying things like, "You don't know anything about anything. You're so stupid."

"Daniel" became so frightening two weeks after we wed that I left the apartment late at night in a cold, heavy rainstorm. I did not want my family to know what was happening because I was embarrassed at being in that situation. So I did not go to one of their homes in the same town. I ended up huddled between two trash dumpsters behind a nearby business, crying. I still remember how lost and hopeless I felt at that moment. My angels came in to comfort me and give me hope. They said that I could leave that marriage and save myself so much pain. Instead, I went back to him.

I was married to this man for ten years. Yes, there were some good times, and my beautiful daughter, Michelle, was a result of that relationship. But his abuse became physical as well as emotional and verbal. Being so beaten down, I saw no way out of the situation. When I talked of leaving, "Daniel" said I was free to go, but I would never see our daughter again. Due to the lengthy, ongoing abuse, I believed him. That threat kept me with him.

Throughout this time, my angels were telling me that I was stronger than I know. They said that I would be able to leave, and though "Daniel" had tried a few times, he would not kill me. Their words sustained me.

Finally, after getting a great job and succeeding in it, I left this man. "Daniel" continued to abuse our daughter and I from a distance until he tragically ended his own life.

Since that ordeal, I have thought about it a great deal. I see how my angels sent "Daniel's" mother and my friend Frank to warn me. They cautioned me and encouraged me to leave. It was my insistence on ignoring my angels and continuing in that toxic marriage that led to ten years of terror and another seven years of his abuse via mail and phone.

It could have been prevented by listening to the wisdom of my angels. I have forgiven myself for this lapse. I cannot change what happened, but I can certainly learn from it. I'd love to say that this lesson was so powerful that I never made a mistake like that again, but that's not true.

Thirteen years later, a second toxic relationship, terrible in a different way, entered my life. This man was "John", whom I mentioned earlier in this book. This time I heard my angels more clearly and often, warning me not to get involved, to walk away. I was sure they were right but came up with all kinds of justification for staying. I had already given up a lot to be with "John". I did not want another failed relationship. Sure, "John" had some great qualities. None of it mattered when compared to the negative aspects.

After that relationship ended, I gave myself a few years to recuperate, reflect and get strong again. Yes, I see that ignoring my angels and doing what I wanted sent me down a dark, destructive path. That toxic relationship was the lesson that brought me to the point of seeing red flags quickly and saying "Next." It was the lesson that got me strong and clear about my mission. I moved to Sedona, worked full time providing spiritual services, and quickly opened my own business with my dear friend, Rozlyn Reynolds.

When I look back at the decisions made at 18 and later in my other toxic relationship, it feels like watching a movie. I cannot fathom why

I kept seeing these noticeably dark people. It is that sensation of being wholly mystified that helped me to forgive myself. I am not who I was at eighteen or even in my forties. These experiences propelled me forward personally and spiritually.

Now, I do not dwell on past mistakes. But I am conscious of having made them and have zero desire to go through another terrible time.

Let's talk about what going rogue means and how to know when you're doing it.

Going What?

When people first used the expression going rogue, it meant 'behaving in an erratic or dangerous fashion." Today, it more often indicates that a person displays independence or fails to follow an expected script. In this book, I'm talking about the latter meaning.

Your angels know the path you have decided for yourself and how best to keep you on it. The expected script is that you will listen to your angels, heed their words by following them.

When you don't know it is your angels speaking to you, it makes it difficult to trust what you're hearing. Doubts can have you wondering if your fears are what you hear. You might push those thoughts aside and continue your course that seems right to you. This kind of confusion happens a lot early in your spiritual journey.

But when you are aware that your angels are talking to you and understand the knowledge they possess about your intended path, your future, and what is happening behind the scenes, it becomes easier to trust them.

Like me, you may not come to this place quickly. It may take you some hard lessons to believe that your angels do know best. And you may be meant to experience at least one hard lesson. Why? Intense challenges help you gain knowledge and insight about yourself.

I'm not alone in ignoring my angel's words and going through difficult times as a result. I'm going to share other people's experiences to understand better what can happen when you go rogue.

A Really Bad Idea

These stories are of people I know personally. Though they gave me permission to share this information, the names have been changed to protect their privacy.

Good for Her, Not for Him

Joan was looking for a new home. Her realtor took her and her husband to see a craftsman-style home. As soon as she walked in, Joan loved that house. She felt welcome and at home from that moment. Her husband did not like the home. He felt uncomfortable in it and did not want to remain inside.

Joan heard her angels saying things like, "This home is not good for you. There is a presence here that will not be good for (her husband)."

She pushed those messages down because she loved that house and was determined to live there.

It did not take long, living in the home, for Joan to realize a male presence there. It wanted her to live there but resented her husband. He never liked the house or felt comfortable in it. Joan eventually felt ambivalence about living there because the spirit hovered too close to her and her husband wanted to move away.

They stayed about a year. During that time, neither Joan nor her husband slept well or felt like it was their home. Joan and her husband decided to sell the home and move, but it cost a lot of time and money to do this.

Having learned a lesson, Joan asked her angels to guide them to a welcoming home for both of them. Their angels pointed them to a new home quickly, where they lived happily for many years.

Darkness Within

Crystal moved to Sedona and wanted to work for a busy shop as a psychic and healer. She had been to this establishment before and enjoyed her time there. She was excited to meet with the owner about renting a room there. As she pulled into the parking lot, she heard her angels say, "Find another place." She took a moment to ask them what the problem was. Her angels said, "Darkness within."

Having been in this place, Crystal did not understand the reference and shrugged it off. She was excited and determined to move ahead with her plan. She rented a room and began seeing customers the next day. Things went well for about a week, but then she began to note some disturbing activities.

She heard one of the employees loudly saying negative things about some of the most ethical, talented psychics working there. A few days later, she noted black magic items displayed in the store. Then one of the other psychics began talking to her about satanism. Being a person of light, Crystal knew she had to leave. She stopped doing readings before her first month ended. She immediately found space in a shop with other people who were of the light.

Crystal said that what she had seen frightened her so badly. She had never been around dark people like that before. She could understand why her angels had warned her away and wished she had listened before joining the business.

To me, the great thing Crystal did was to see that she made a mistake and leave as quickly as possible. We're only human. We will make bad choices. But if you can recognize them and rectify them right away, you cannot go too far off course.

I reconnected with Crystal a few years later. She was working at another establishment and enjoying it. As she told me, the people at the new place were friendly, supportive, and full of light. During her first week there, she realized how negatively the previous business had impacted her. Her spiritual gifts became more refined, which improved the quality of her readings and healings. Most important was that Crystal felt happier with much less stress.

She said that she had no regrets about leaving the other shop except that she had not gone sooner. But she did leave, and that's what is crucial in a situation like this. Had she stayed, she risked having her energy dramatically depleted, feeling depressed, having her gifts blocked, and losing income.

Choose a Different Partner

Bill was ready to expand his business and needed a partner to handle some aspects of the company that was not his strength. After meeting with a few candidates, he decided to bring Matthew in as his partner. He felt drawn to Matthew and saw that Matthew had skills that would help propel the business to the next level.

Many of Bill's family and circle of friends who met Matthew offered caution about going into business with this man. Some said they did not trust him. Others said they couldn't put their finger on it but keep looking. Choose a different partner, some said.

This shocked and upset Bill as he could not understand what they saw that he did not. Bill admits that he had a nagging doubt about Matthew, but he was so relieved to find someone with Matthew's skills that he pushed it aside. Bill had heard thoughts like, "Look deeper" and "Not this man." He had attributed those thoughts to his cautious nature.

He did bring Bill in as a partner, and things were good for nearly a year. Matthew handled accounts receivable and payable, freeing Bill to seek new clients and give more attention to their existing clientele.

A supplier contacted Bill complaining that Bill's company had not paid the supplier. They also said that Matthew was not returning calls. They were angry and wanted answers. Bill looked into the books that night, after hours, and discovered multiple large supplier invoices that were unpaid and overdue.

Bill asked Matthew why he was not paying these bills. Matthew always had an explanation, but it just did not add up. Bill knew there was plenty of money coming in to keep up with the bills.

Those negative comments his family and friends had made about Matthew were going around and around in his head. He felt alarm bells going off about the situation. Bill decided to take a deeper look into the business' accounting records. He saw that payments were being made regularly to a company he did not recognize.

These payments had started nine months earlier in smaller amounts. Each month, the amount had gone up. Now the total sent to this company had left them unable to pay their supplier bills. The evidence was clear. Matthew was stealing from the business.

The next day, he presented Matthew with the evidence and had charges filed against Matthew. Bill felt betrayed and blindsided. But after his first session with me, the more he thought about the situation, the clearer he could see that he had received warning messages from his angels and those who love and care about him. It was not that Bill had caught by surprise. He had chosen to ignore his angels for expediency.

I encouraged Bill not to beat himself up about what had happened. He learned to focus on the lessons he learned. Yes, he had a debt to work his way through. And he had damaged business relationships to heal. Bill put his energy into undoing the mess his former partner had created. Shortly after we met, he found a great business partner, and the company has been thriving since then.

Wondering if you are in a dark night of the soul, or have been ever?

Keep reading to learn the signs.

Dark Night of the Soul

A Spanish monk named Saint John of the Cross, coined the term "Dark Night of the Soul." The name of his poem is "Noche Oscura," based on his own mystical experience.

You should know that a Dark Night of the Soul is a stage in your spiritual evolution. It happens to you when you are a highly evolved human at a pivotal point in your spiritual development. It is a milestone in your soul's evolution. When a rupture forms between your past and present, circumstances tend to be drastic. It is a period of great emotional pain, confusion, and despair. Your life is turned upside down and maybe even inside out.

Later you will recognize that everything in your life before this time was preparing you for a challenge. It's time you set aside so that you may enter into this higher chapter of your life. It's rather like March; "In like a lion, out like a lamb." A Dark Night of the Soul pounces upon you, unexpected, unwanted. It is ferocious and unrelenting. When it ends, you are a different person. You can see your life more clearly, discard experiences, gather lessons, and recognize that this new you is vastly different from how you were before. You make a tremendous leap forward in your development.

When in this state, you don't realize that your past is truly gone. You push to return to who you were and the life you had. It can't happen because you are supposed to move forward. This process is most traumatic.

It's not uncommon for you to feel, on some level, that you are going to die. This sensation is symbolic of the death of your earlier life and the birth of a new life you cannot begin to perceive. You feel cast adrift, lost, hopeless. It seems there is no way out, but that is because you are trying to move backward.

Again, the only path open for you is forward. The only way to reach the point of having a Dark Night of the Soul is through dedication to spirituality, God, Source, and striving to be a better person. A limitation you carry within is put right in front of your face. It's impossible not to look at it, examine it. It's hard to see a fault you have carried through many lifetimes. But when you have a Dark Night of the Soul, it's time for you to see the limitation that's been holding you back, acknowledge it, and leave it behind.

It is utter torture to be in this state because everything within goes dark. You feel dead inside, numb and lost. The mind projects that state outward to one believe the entire world and every person on the planet is as lost as you feel. It's as if there is not one thing you can hold onto for assurance. There's no consolation for you. All you feel is emptiness and hopelessness. It's these feelings that lead many to contemplate suicide. But acting on that would nullify the immense spiritual shift you are getting reach to experience.

When you are in a Dark Night of the Soul, you may feel a disconnection from your Higher Power. It is as if God simply becomes an idea. It's not that you stop believing in God, but more that you may feel God is not reaching out to you. You know there is a God but think that God is not hearing you or caring about your difficult situation. You may feel that God has become indifferent to you and the suffering you endure.

This situation brings about a condition that is not life and also not death. It's a terrible void where you simply exist. Within this condition, there is only stagnation, a feeling of abandonment.

Now you know what a Dark Night of the Soul is. Keep reading to learn how to recognize when you, or someone you care about, is in this state.

Signs You Are in One

The specifics of what happened can vary greatly. But the signs that you are in a Dark Night of the Soul are relatively consistent. Here are some clues you may see exhibited:

- Depression
- Hopelessness
- Health issues
- Inability to focus
- Difficulty working
- Reduced income
- Insomnia
- Fear or anxiety
- Unable to take action
- Suicidal ideation

There are other signs, but these are the primary ones. Put a small check next to every sign you see happening now in yourself and your life. If you have five or more checks, you are likely in a Dark Night of the Soul. The odds are that you knew you were in a terrible place before you read this book. You may not have called it anything specific but feeling miserable with your life is easy to identify.

It's not unusual to get stuck in this dark mess. The hopelessness alone makes it so difficult to see a way out. Avoid isolating so you do not miss out on receiving input from those in a better emotional place who could help you.

If you let this go on too long, you put yourself at risk for severe health issues, losing your job, losing your housing, losing friends, becoming mired in fear, losing trust in God and your angels, and even coming to a place where you see no way out except taking your life.

It does not have to be like this. Know that the longer you let it go on, the worse it gets. You cannot pull yourself out of this alone. You can take some steps, but you will need assistance if you want to turn this around.

Let's go over how to get out of a Dark Night of the Soul. I'm going to share some steps with you that will help you as quickly as possible.

Out of the Pit

This terrible situation does not have you trapped. It may feel like it, but you do have choices. Here's the thing about options; sometimes they are tough to make. Choices can be scary and daunting. But seeing that you always have choices is empowering for you. When you are down this low, you need to build your inner strength back up. That is done step-by-step.

The first step is to get up, take a shower, wash the negativity off from within and without. Dress in something that makes you feel good.

Take ten long, deep breaths. Visualize that every breath in is pulling energy and power from the Universe, filling your lungs and entire body with strength. With every breath in, feel your energy rise and grow.

Out loud, ask your angels to intervene on your behalf and help you create the life you desire. Be specific with what your ideal life is. Then spend a few minutes seeing that life that you do want to experience. See your desired life in as much detail as possible.

Pick up the phone and call a person who loves or cares about you. Tell them what you have been going through and ask if they can help you. Be prepared to let them know how they can best help you. Often people want to help but don't know what to do. Accept the assistance offered to you. Isolation will only prolong this state. Allow those who care about you to help lift you out of the pit.

Earlier in this book, I talked about how my friend, Brian, called me nightly to check in on me. He was soothing, reassuring and so patient. Most importantly, he listened. I felt heard and knew I wasn't alone with this situation.

Take one action toward making your life better. For instance, if you went through a toxic relationship that led to your Dark Night of the Soul, make a list of the red flags you saw early on with that person. It might be something they said, did, or a reaction. When you have that list done, tape it on your bathroom mirror. You will be referring to it later when you begin dating again. It will be your early-warning system. Rather than getting into another toxic relationship, make a pact with yourself if a date exhibits one or more items on your red flat list but will say "next" and move on.

Every time your mind goes to fear, anger or sadness, ask yourself, "What do I need right now?" Re-focusing on yourself and your needs of the moment helps you to get centered and balanced again. If you need a nap and can take one, do it. Perhaps you need more water or some lounging in a hammock, meditation, or time in nature. If you cannot give yourself what you need at that moment, do it as soon as possible.

Do forgiveness work on yourself. You likely made some choices you regret, did not respond the way you wish you had or allowed things to continue too long. You are human. You will make mistakes. Forgive yourself and determine to make better, healthier choices going forward. You will find a powerful, effective Forgiveness prayer on my website under the Resources tab. I did not write it, but I've been using it for myself and clients for years. It works.

Take some time to write down the lessons and wisdom you learned through the experience you went through. Out of the deepest dark come points of light that help us expand, shift forward and even find our life purpose. Finding those positive outcomes and realizing that the negative experience you went through brought those outcomes into your life helps change your perspective. Perhaps your adversity propelled you to your life purpose faster than you would have got there without it. It may have yanked you from a path you were determined to walk and put you firmly on your intended life course.

Attend a CoDA (Codependents Anonymous) meeting. They are offered virtually as well as in person. CoDA is a 12-step group for codependents. "Codependency is a circular relationship in which one person needs the other person, who in turn needs to be needed. The codependent person, known as 'the giver,' feels worthless unless needed by, and making sacrifices for, the enabler, otherwise known as 'the taker,' according to author Dr. Renee Exelberg in a post on VeryWellMind.com Lightworkers are prone to codependent relationships. You will gain a lot of insight into your past and tools for moving forward in relationships from romantic to work and family.

Perhaps you think you are not a codependent. Maybe not, but if you allowed yourself to be abused in any way, you will learn tools at CoDA meetings that will help you set healthy boundaries. Your relationships will be better moving forward.

Practice gratitude. Every morning and night, state three things you are grateful for out loud. When you begin this, it may be basic blessings that come to mind, such as "I'm grateful to have a roof over my head." As you heal, you will see more of the blessings you have in your life, such as "I'm grateful for my friends." Focusing on the good aspects of your life helps pull you further up out of the pit.

Remember I said you wouldn't be able to do this on your own. To avoid falling back down or becoming isolated again, you need to find your tribe. I'm going to tell you how to achieve that in the next section.

Find a Spiritual Circle.

When you are feeling more like yourself again, it's time to find your tribe. These are the people with who you feel comfortable around. You are on a spiritual journey. It's likely that you are well aware of this and seeking information. It can be lonely when you don't have people to talk to about your experiences, thoughts, and plans. Many don't have one person on a similar path and interested in talking about the things you wish to discuss.

A fast way to find a circle is through www.Meetup.com. Enter the term "Spirituality" and how far you are willing to travel to attend a meeting. This website is the modern equivalent of perusing index cards pinned to a bulletin board in metaphysical shops.

Yep, that's how we did it in the '70s into the '90s. Quaint, isn't it? A variety of options are available on Meetup.com. Visit the ones that appeal to you a few times to get a good idea of the membership. If there isn't one in your area, consider starting one. I did that twice when I was in that situation. It can take a while to attract a true circle. It may be just you and one or two others for a time. So you form more of a spiritual line than a circle for a while. That's fine. These meetings can be purely social, centered around a specific topic, have guest speakers, and other formats.

A spiritual circle is an essential part of:

- Getting stronger
- Staying strong
- Feeling like you fit in
- Being heard
- Learning something new

- Sharing experiences

- Keeping you on track spiritually and emotionally

When you begin to see your angels, you are going to be excited. You'll want to tell someone. Uncle Bob might look at you like you just announced you are joining a circus. But a spiritual circle will be thrilled for you. They will want to hear all about it. Chances are they will share their visions with you.

It's great to have like-minded friends to talk with about the messages you get from your angels, the signs you see, what you've learned about Angel Numbers, and your desired life path.

You do not have to travel this road alone, and it's detrimental to try. The Dark Night of the Soul is not what led to your issues. It's more likely that your gifts made life harder on you. Being an Empath is rough when you don't know how to shield.

Here are some exercises which will help you feel better about yourself and gain more confidence in your ability to discern angelic messages and signs.

Exercises

Be Your Best Friend

Think of the rough situation you experienced. Come up with at least one way you had a part in its creation. Ask yourself what your best friend or a supportive family member would say to you about it. When you have their words in your head, repeat them a few times. If you have difficulty with this, ask your best friend or loved one directly how they see the issue.

Take note of the love, care, gentle approach, and understanding they exhibit toward you. When thoughts like that come to your mind again, recall the more loving words about yourself. Let this be your new narrative.

The Do-Good List

You are probably carrying a list of your mistakes and "should haves" in your head. Make a point of noting when you do something which you perceive as positive. Please write it down on a list and post it. Look at that list every morning and every night.

You make some good decisions, and your mind needs reminders. Your good choices help to counter the not-so-good ones. Focus on those good ones and visualize letting the negative ones roll off you as if angels dipped you in Rain-X.

Own Your Decisions

Be a person of your word. Consider a little longer before making decisions. Some decisions are rough, choosing between the proverbial rock and a hard place. Yet, it would be best if you made a decision. Putting it off can make things worse. Delaying a decision weighs on your mind and reduces your focus.

When you do make a decision, own it. Let the decisions you make reflect the person you want to be. This process is something you do throughout every day going forward. Be ready to accept the results of your decisions.

Remind yourself that you chose to do something because you felt it was the best option. Each decision you make will help you feel more secure about making the next one.

Connect to your Higher Power

You can do this through prayer, meditation, journaling, visualization, spending quiet time in nature, singing, or making music. Now is a great time to deepen your connection to deepen your connection to God; your

Higher Power. Sometimes going through an extremely trying time can lead you to feel forsaken or not seen by God's eye. God/Source sees you. You are important. Reinforcing this relationship can do wonders for filling in the holes in your heart and soul left by trauma.

If you choose to spend quiet time in nature, it is best if you do this alone. This time in nature needs to be contemplative. I always feel closest to God when I'm outdoors. Look at the natural beauty around you. Notice the whole scene and the small details such as tiny wildflowers or sunlight filtering through the green leaves of a tree. Close your eyes and feel the energy of that location. Visualize it moving up through the soles of your feet. Feel that energy moving up through your body until it stops at the top of your head. Hold that energy within and let it invigorate you.

Now that you have some tools for making your way out of a Dark Night of the Soul, I want to share what happens when you are in dire need and call upon your angels for assistance.

CHAPTER FOURTEEN
Parade of Angels

Spectacular Protection

During the worst times in the toxic relationship, I mentioned earlier, I began to see angels in a new way for me. I remember being in bed, crying softly, and feeling hopeless. As I lay in there in the dark, eyes open, an angel came in from the right side of my bed. It came right through the wall into my room. This angel showed me its beautiful, radiant colors and covered me in its high-frequency energy. That angel passed through me, and another angel was right behind it. I was astonished and felt like I was witnessing a miracle.

This breathtaking display went on for about two hours. I knew I was experiencing something sacred and meaningful. As they continued to appear, one after another, each with its dazzling colors, I felt better. Eventually, a deep sense of peace and love filled my being. I felt lifted above my relationship situation. My previous worry and anxiety were gone. I heard them saying that all would be well. It was such a relief on every level. The appearance of this line of angels went on until I fell asleep.

I call this experience a "Parade of Angels." They showed me hundreds of angels coming in to let me know the level of divine protection I had at that time. I clung to the knowledge that so many angels cared about my welfare and were doing what they could to help me. This dazzling display happened a few times in my last year of that damaging relationship. I credit that spectacular level of protection for my survival and ability to shift forward in creating the life I wanted.

Let's talk about when to ask for angelic intervention.

Crisis Assistance

There are times when you are not able to handle a situation. You can feel so low mentally and emotionally that you cannot come up with a plan. It could be that the problem is totally out of your hands; nothing you do will make a difference. Another reason is that you are frozen in fear, afraid to make a move or decide anything. You could be in actual danger and need serious assistance. These are examples but not all-inclusive. If you feel like you can't handle the situation or have no idea what to do, it's time to ask your angels to intervene.

Being stuck does not have to be a life-or-death event. It can be a more mundane issue that you have been unable to develop a way to overcome. If this has gone on for a while, again, it's time to go to your angels.

Here are some examples of situations where you will benefit from asking your angels to intervene:

- Being in an abusive relationship (physically, verbally, emotionally, or mentally)
- Experiencing severe pain for an extended period
- Facing a life-threatening diagnosis
- The loss of a loved one who you were close with
- Feeling lost in your life

- Being unable to decide on an important issue
- Severe fear
- Loss of a job
- Financial stress
- Inability to forgive
- Being affected by acts of God (flood, tornado, etc.)

Indeed, there are other times when you will feel so overwhelmed that you cannot move forward without the intervention of your angels. The above list is not all-inclusive.

How do you ask for that extra assistance? I'm going to share that with you now.

Requesting Help

You will be asking for help from your angels. Doing so is the best place to begin because your angels are focused solely on you. They have the most time and energy to devote to assisting you.

Sit with legs uncrossed and both feet on the floor. Your arms uncrossed, palms facing up. Out loud, say, "Angels, please intervene on my behalf and (insert the specific need you have)." That word "intervene" is essential as it signals to your angels that you are in dire need of immediate assistance. It gets their attention fast. Repeat this daily until an intervention occurs.

Release expectations of immediate results. In my experience, the results of this request can take from a day to months to occur. Your angels hear your request at the time you make it. They are then busy behind the scenes fulfilling your request. We cannot know what that entails, so it's best to be as patient as you can. Know that your angels are on the job, helping you before you can even see the results.

It's possible to see divine protection. Let's talk about what you may see.

Seeing Angelic Protection

I first saw angelic protection when I was in my second Dark Night of the Soul. They knew how hopeless I was feeling. Showing me their presence instantly put a spark of hope in my heart. My spirits lifted and I felt loved and guarded.

You read my story about the first time I saw a Parade of Angels. I know my angels were working hard to help me, but I was sinking fast. They sent me hundreds of angels, one after another, showing me the high level of protection that I was being given. It allowed me to sleep better, trust that the situation I was in would end and my life would return to one of joy. But that's just one sign of the protection your angels are providing to you.

Another is a massive flash of white light. I had moved to Sedona and was working on my computer in my bedroom with the lights turned off. Suddenly a huge white flash lit up my room.

I saw it as a reflection on my computer monitor. The entire room was more visible than it was midday with the curtains open. I gasped and turned away from my computer. I saw the room very bright and then it was gone. Seconds later, I was back in a darkened room. I felt the frequency of many angels lingering around me. I never knew why they sent that powerful flash of light. I can only imagine that I was an unknown danger. I thanked them for watching over me.

I realized that I had seen that same big flash of white light multiple times in the early '90s when I was a single parent living in Prescott, Arizona. At that time, my mind tried to talk me out of having seen something angelic or even paranormal. But I did wake up to very bright flashes of light like that several times. Even then, my angels were showing me that I was not alone. That everything would be okay. Sadly, I missed out on knowing that.

Another sign you may see is a wide arc of white light. When I lived in a house with a lot of paranormal activity and was under attack by some dark people, I began seeing this beautiful sign of divine protection. I'd be in bed, seeing flashlights shining in the window of my back door, hearing people walking outside my home. A silent, side arc of white light would start at the left side of my room and make its way to the right side. With it came very high-frequency energy and such calm.

It sounds odd to go from being terrified to going to sleep, but this sign of my angels protecting me allowed me to do that. You can only go so long without some decent sleep. I did not see this arc every night, but it was often enough to give me courage in the face of danger.

Let's move on to some exercises that will help you shift out of fear and stress and into joy.

Exercises

Here are some great suggestions you can do yourself. The following exercises are based on a post on Bustle.com:

<u>Deep Breathing</u>

Sit comfortably, tune into the emotion that's bothering you. Breathe in through your nose and release that breath slowly through your mouth. It's helpful to visualize the feeling as a color. As you breathe out, "see" that color leaving your body and dissipating harmlessly into the Universe. Do 10, or more, of these long releasing breaths,

<u>Write it Out</u>

Writing can be cathartic. When you feel emotions that you don't want to share with someone else, share them in your journal. Putting your feelings into words has been found to alleviate pain. This process is helpful because writing about them reduces your emotional response in the amygdala part of your brain.

Stop and Distract

Distraction can be a great way to prevent yourself from thinking negative thoughts or dwelling on a negative situation. You can control your emotions. When you first realize you feel a negative emotion, say "Stop!" in your head. Then distract yourself by engaging in an activity you enjoy or starting something new and fun. This distraction will help you push through unwanted emotions.

Workout

An aerobic workout that helps release emotions trapped in your body by getting your heart pumping. Aerobic exercise works well for:

- Neck and back pain
- Stiff muscles
- Headaches

A combination of meditation and aerobic exercise is helpful in reducing:

- Depression
- Negative thoughts
- "Monkey mind", which is persistent thoughts that run around and around in your mind. Often they disrupt sleep

Imagery

This works great for dispelling anger. Imagine your anger as red hot lava. See yourself pouring refreshing cool water over that lava. See that cooled lava in your mind and imagine kicking it way out into space. Imagine it moving further away until you cannot see it anymore. Let yourself feel the absence of anger.

Smiling

Just trying to be positive can help. Take a walk in a public place where you are sure to see other people. Smile at each one. Say "hello" and smile. This small act releases negative energy. When you are feeling down, smiling can create a feedback loop effect on your body. It causes a release of the positive emotions you want to feel.

Sleep

Getting seven to nine hours of sleep per night gives you a solid emotional baseline so you can handle difficult emotions. Your sleep is about more than feeling rested. It can help reset your brain's ability to cope with emotions. This reset allows your ongoing response to adverse situations. Go to bed and wake up at the same time every day to improve the quality of your sleep.

Fountain of Joy

Once you have left overwhelming negative emotions behind, you can benefit from consciously increasing the joy in your life. Here are some exercises to help you with this, based on a post on tinybuddha.com:

Three Funny Things

Write down three funny things you experienced recently. Include whether you were directly involved in the event, you observed it, or did it happen spontaneously? Let yourself be in the moment that each event occurred. Feel laughter bubbling up and let it out. Laughing lifts your mood instantly and leads to more laughter

Conscious Acts of Kindness

The connections you have to other people are oxygen to your sense of well-being. Nurturing your current relationships and seeking new ones will fuel your happiness. An excellent way to begin is to consciously reach out to someone and share a positive thought or experience with them.

Every morning, make a point of emailing someone to write something positive or praise them sincerely for their contributions to your life. Giving mindful attention to your social relationships creates more positive habits in your routine, deepens your connections, and provides you with a cushion from the toxic impact of stress.

You now know how to build a loving, meaningful relationship with your angels. Also, you have gained a lot of tools to help you improve your angelic communication abilities and assist you in experiencing more divine events. The only thing left is to give you some parting words.

Dear Reader

Know that you are a huge part of your angels' being, especially your Master Guide and Guardian Angel who took sacred vows to guide and protect you. Bonding with your angels simply means making angels a bigger part of your daily life. You started that journey by reading this book. Remember to talk with them as you go through your days. Keep in mind that your angels are near you always.

My hope for you is that you implement the skills you learned in this book into your life so that you will enjoy an increase in divine guidance and angelic intercession. Also, you can expect to have more feelings of safety, love, peace, and calm.

If you want to learn more about your angels now, I can help you with that. It will be helpful for you to know the names, appearances, and messages from your angels as early into your journey as possible. Often, simply learning this information pulls down a barrier within you, allowing you to move forward faster in having the meaningful relationship with your angels that you desire. When you're ready to learn, visit my website for more information on a Meet Your Angelic Guides session.

Celestial Connections

- (1) LearnReligions.com, Simple Chakracises, By Phylameana lila Desy, Updated May 09, 2019

- Love You Inside Out, by the BeeGees

- http://sacredscribesangelnumbers.blogspot.com/p/index-numbers.html, by Joanne Walmsley, 2000

- https://www.verywellmind.com/what-is-codependency-5072124; by Wendy Rose Gould, Updated on December 08, 2020

- https://www.bustle.com/articles/151298-8-healthy-ways-to-release-negative-emotion-so-youhttps://www.bustle.com/articles/151298-8-healthy-ways-to-release-negative-emotion-so-you-can-feel-better-the-right-waycan-feel-better-the-right-way ; by Carina Wolff, March 31, 2016

- https://tinybuddha.com/blog/6-exercises-positive-psychology-boost-happiness/; by Linda Esposito, 2016

Contact Ivory LaNoue

Email- ivoryangelic@outlook.com

Phone- 844-811-1195 (toll-free)

Book Website: https://ivorylanoue.com/

Main Website: https://ivoryangelicmedium.com/

Courses & Classes Website: https://spiritualitydevelopment.com/

Ivory's Podcast: The Angel Room

Podcast Website: https://theangelroompodcast.com/

YouTube Channel: Ivory LaNoue

Instagram: ivorylanoueaz

About the Author

Ivory LaNoue is a respected angel communicator, psychic medium, spiritual counselor and mentor based in central Arizona.

She has connected thousands of people around the world with their angels. Ivory enjoys teaching and speaking about angels, other spiritual topics, and personal growth.

When she's not doing her spiritual work, Ivory is playing harp and other musical instruments, singing at various venues, gardening, reading, and enjoying time with friends and family.

Learn more about her at IvoryAngelicMedium.com.

Printed in Great Britain
by Amazon